# THE KNIGHTED SKIES

*A Pictorial History of World War I in the Air*

Other books by the same author:

*The Gershwin Years*, with Lawrence D. Stewart

*Harold Arlen: Happy With the Blues*

*George Gershwin*

*B-17, the Story of the Flying Fortress*

# THE KNIGHTED SKIES

*A Pictorial History*
*of World War I in the Air*

by

Edward Jablonski

THOMAS NELSON & SONS LTD

Copyright © 1964 by Edward Jablonski

THOMAS NELSON AND SONS LTD

36 Park Street London W1
Parkside Works Edinburgh 9
10 Warehouse Road Lagos Apapa

THOMAS NELSON (AUSTRALIA) Ltd
117 Latrobe Street Melbourne C1

THOMAS NELSON AND SONS (AFRICA) (Pty) LTD
P.O. Box 9881 Johannesburg

THOMAS NELSON AND SONS (CANADA) LTD
81 Curlew Drive Don Mills Ontario

THOMAS NELSON AND SONS
Copewood and Davis Streets Camden 3, N.J.

SOCIÉTÉ FRANÇAISE D'ÉDITIONS NELSON
97 rue Monge Paris 5

———

*First published 1964*

*Printed in the United States of America*

# For Edith

*They are the knighthood of this war, with-
out fear and without reproach; and they
recall the legendary days of chivalry, not
merely by the daring of their exploits, but
by the nobility of their spirit.*

—DAVID LLOYD-GEORGE

# Contents

# *Foreword*

The war in the air fought during 1914-1918 was unique. It had never happened before and was never to happen again. The men who participated in this new form of warfare lived—and died—as had no other men before in history. It was this singularity which undoubtedly rendered them so fascinating to mere groundlings and which attracted so much attention to them. They were, most of them, very young and their youth was as much a part of their armament as the planes they flew and the guns they fired.

It should be recalled that their weapons, however unpredictable, were the most modern conceived up to that time. Only in retrospect could the wonderful Nieuports, Fokkers, Spads, "Camels" and S. E. 5s be looked upon as "crates." In the brief span of four years the advances in the design of aircraft and engines were remarkable; that too is a part of the story.

Most of it, however, belongs to the men who flew these little planes (there were large planes, too, but they were never as romantic as the single-seaters). Certain that they engaged in the most dangerous, yet most glorious, means of making war, the airmen visualized themselves as beings apart from those who struggled in the mud below. They accumulated, and invented, their own traditions and even a folklore. It is believed that these first air fighters fought according to a code of the air, a modern equivalent to the old precepts of chivalry. To some extent this is true, for during the early months of the war a curious comradeship arose between the airmen of the warring nations. Understanding each other's peculiar problems in connection with getting an erratic machine off the ground and keeping it there, they eventually developed a tradition of, whenever possible, giving an enemy pilot a "sporting chance." It would seem that if men could kill according to "civilized" rules, they could agree not to kill at all. But that was not part of the game and no one recognized the grand hypocrisy at the time. On the other hand, there were men who fought only according to the rules of war, leaving no romantic loopholes in a deadly game. They were the realists and, it might be said, they were in the majority.

At this latter day the stories of these last knights are thrice-told tales. But for all that, they continue to be fascinating. Almost equally so are the hundreds of photographs that were taken of them and their aircraft. Up to its time, the First World War was the most photographed conflict in history. Unfortunately, aerial photography was in its infancy and air-to-air photographs were a rarity. Combat shots were practically nonexistent. It may be stressed here that all photographs used in this book are authentic, most of them chosen from the archives of the various nations involved. The only questionable air-to-air photographs are those from the controversial Cockburn-Lange collection which were supposedly actually taken in combat. There are those who say these photographs were faked (using carefully built models) and there are those who insist they are genuine. True or false, the photographs do capture the feel of air combat and are interesting in themselves. Personally, I am inclined to feel that the Cockburn-Lange photographs are not authentic.

As for the other, unquestionably genuine, photographs I am indebted to a number of collectors and agencies who made possible a choice of shots that help to round out the story of the men and machines of the first war in the air.

Col. G. B. Jarrett placed his entire collection of World War I photographs at my disposal (only a third of which appear here). As a historian, Colonel Jarrett has collected material pertaining to the air war for two or three decades and his vast collection is as comprehensive as it is excellent. Throughout the writing of this book, and even before, Colonel Jarrett was encouraging and helpful. Without his generous and unselfish help, many a fine illustration would have been lacking from these pages.

My friend, Lt. Col. Gene Guerny, of the U. S. Air Force's outstanding Book Program, furnished me with his usual good-natured aid and wise counsel. He also placed the Air Force's file of historic photographs at my disposal. Another friend, Royal D. Frey of the Air Force Museum at Wright-Patterson Air Force Base, Ohio, provided me with ideas, insights and the loan of several World War I aircraft rigging manuals. The treatment afforded by the Air Force to writers, historians and scholars is one of the rare pleasurable experiences of working in this field.

Other sources which furnished quick and ready aid are the Air Museum of the Smithsonian Institution; the National Archives; the Imperial War Museum, London; *Etablissement Cinématographique des Armées,* Fort D'Ivry, France, and the Canadian Department of National Defence, Royal Canadian Air Force.

I am also deeply indebted to Mr. D. Jay Culver and Mr. Sol Novin, of Culver Pictures. Not only was I given access to the wide resources of the Culver Picture collection, but was also given a good deal of help in the handling of problem photographs. It may be that selling pictures is Mr. Culver's business, but he has managed to make it a pleasure as well as an art.

Personal interviews with Mr. Walter Chalaire, Mr. Reed Chambers and Mr. George A. Vaughn, Jr.—all, of course, ex-World War I pilots—enabled me to absorb some of the atmosphere and the "feel" of air fighting as well as to check upon, first hand, certain legends of the time. However much myth-making there was during the war, these men most certainly sustain the truth that they were gentlemen in those days. They still are.

My editor, Miss Carol Sturm, has been a kindly, concerned and discreet guiding light throughout the overlong period of the writing and compilation of this book. She even managed to make sense of some pretty convoluted sentences, not to mention some spelling that could only be described as gauche. Putnam's brilliant young editor in chief, Peter Israel, was a fine champion from the very beginning. It was at this point, luckily, that he had suggestions to make and ideas to offer—all of which were readily adapted.

My friend Joseph F. Elder, of the Scott Meredith Literary Agency, was also most important in the final form this book took. He is a most patient, and perceptive, sounding board whose help goes beyond the expected.

And, finally, I must admit that the book's title was not conceived by me but by Putnams' Walter Minton. In my opinion it is the best writing in the book.

—E. J.

New York
*May 1964*

# THE KNIGHTED SKIES

*A Pictorial History of World War I in the Air*

# Prelude

*. . . we at once packed our goods and re-turned home, knowing that the age of the flying machine had come at last.*

—WILBUR AND ORVILLE WRIGHT

At Kitty Hawk, North Carolina, December 17, 1903           U. S. AIR FORCE

# Man left the earth

in controlled, powered flight for the first time on December 17, 1903, at Kitty Hawk, North Carolina. At the controls of an ungainly-looking contraption of wood, wire and fabric was Orville Wright, a builder of bicycles from Dayton, Ohio. Witnessing this historic event—one of the few epochal moments in history completely ignored by the press—were Wilbur Wright, Orville's brother and partner in the invention, plus five men and a boy. This, of course, suited the diffident, secretive Wrights for they preferred the seclusion afforded by Kitty Hawk, located in a remote coastal section between Albemarle Sound and the Atlantic Ocean. There too they found wide beaches, sand dunes and steady winds.

Though neither Orville nor Wilbur were engineers or scientists, an early interest in flight, sparked by the gift of a flying toy from their father when they were boys, led them to read widely in the burgeoning literature on the subject. They read avidly of the gliding exploits of the German Otto Lilienthal who, in the 1890's, made thousands of flights in a glider of his own design from a hill near Berlin. "Flying creatures," Lilienthal said, "and especially birds, demonstrate that travel through the air is far more perfect than all other means of travel. Natural bird flight utilizes the properties of the air. . . ." Lilienthal's theories, so dramatically demonstrated in his flights, were widely read and influential, particularly his book *Experiments in Soaring*. His death as the result of a glider accident in 1896 did not lessen his influence on future aeronautical pioneers, among them the Wright brothers. Theirs was not an accidental discovery but one resulting from a long line of antecedents:

> We then studied with great interest Chanute's *Progress in Flying Machines,* Langley's *Experiments in Aerodynamics,* the *Aeronautical Annuals* of 1896, and 1897, and several pamphlets published by the Smithsonian Institution, especially articles by Lilienthal and extracts from Mouillard's *Empire of the Air*. The larger works gave us a good understanding of the nature of the flying problem and the difficulties in past attempts to solve it, while Mouillard and Lilienthal, the great missionaries of the flying cause, infected us with their own unquenchable enthusiasm, and transformed idle curiosity into the active zeal of workers.

The great contribution of the Wright brothers to "the flying problem" was the idea of adding power to convert gliders into a modern aircraft. There being no engine available at the time which combined the right power and lightness, the Wrights characteristically went about designing their own. Experimentation with their own homemade wind tunnel, their own carefully made computations, their ability as mechanics, plus an amazing scientific instinct combined to produce the craft in which man would first actually fly.

As Orville, who piloted the plane, was to recall later:

3

Orville Wright, in the improved Type "A" biplane, preparing for takeoff as part of the demonstration for the Signal Corps                    U. S. AIR FORCE

The course of the flight up and down was exceedingly erratic, partly due to the irregularity of the air, and partly to lack of experience in handling this machine. . . . This flight lasted only 12 seconds, but it was nevertheless the first in the history of the world in which a machine carrying a man had raised itself by its own power into the air in full flight, had sailed forward without the reduction of speed, and had finally landed at a point as high as that from which it started.

This cautious, and for the Wrights characteristic language was necessary if the real contribution of the brothers is to be understood. They were not, of course, the first men to leave the ground in a man-made contraption. The Montgolfier brothers in France had accomplished this as early as 1783 in a balloon (an event enthusiastically reported by Benjamin Franklin); birdlike men with wings glided from the tops of hills into valleys below them (and sometimes to their deaths) in the nineteenth century. But no one before the Wright brothers had ever, as reported in one newspaper, "flown three miles in a box kite."

The persevering Wrights, heartened by this short flight and others of longer duration made that same day until the wind damaged their plane, continued to improve their machine. They refined the control system and they experimented with improved engines and were successful in all areas except one: they could not interest anyone in high position, not even their own government, in their invention.

4

Orville Wright has been taken out of the wreck of his aircraft (far right) and spectators are attempting to remove Lt. Thomas Selfridge from the plane; Selfridge was fatally injured in the crash                    U. S. AIR FORCE

The Wright Type "A" biplane in flight, Fort Myer, Virginia          U. S. AIR FORCE

Not until 1908, after five years of discouragement, were the Wrights able to convince the War Department of their *Flyer*'s potential as a military device —and this, only after President Theodore Roosevelt intervened. Meanwhile, during this same period of American inertia, the Wrights' machine inspired European aeronauts to design their own flying machines patterned after and improving upon the *Flyer*.

During September 1908, Orville Wright demonstrated the improved Type "A" biplane for the War Department at Fort Myer, Virginia. By this time an Aeronautical Division, for some reason a branch of the Signal Corps, had been established. It was to "have charge of all matters pertaining to military ballooning, air machines, and all kindred subjects." In charge of this new division was Capt. Charles DeForest Chandler, whose total staff consisted of Cpl. Edward Ward and Pfc. Joseph E. Barrett.

The new Wright plane easily fulfilled the qualifications specified by the War Department: it carried not only the pilot but also a passenger; it attained a speed of at least 40 mph and could carry enough fuel to make a flight of 125 miles. On September 17, 1908, on the last flight of a series of tests, a cracked propeller caught in a brace wire and threw the *Flyer* out of control. The plane fell to the ground, seriously injuring Orville Wright and killing his passenger, Lt. Thomas E. Selfridge. Not until August 2 of the following year did the Wright brothers receive a government contract, whereupon their Type A aircraft became the first military plane in history.

Alberto Santos-Dumont and his plane "14 *bis*," November 1906, about to make his first public flight with an aircraft in Europe. The "14 *bis*" flew tail first

AIR FRANCE

Louis Blériot at the finish of his cross-channel flight, July 25, 1909. The landing wiped out the plane's landing gear and broke the propeller, but Blériot was unhurt. In the background the land of Dover Castle rises out of Northfall Meadow

Almost from the moment he ascended into the air, man, with an uncanny instinct for self-destruction, began to dream of using this new dimension militarily. As early as June 2, 1794, the French had employed hydrogen-filled balloons at Maubeuge for observation with possibly the most effective use at the Battle of Fleurus later in the month. Napoleon, a traditionalist for all his military genius, disbanded the French balloon companies in 1799. In 1805 one French artist-militarist envisioned a cross-Channel invasion of England by means of balloons plus a tunnel under the English Channel. The French, he imagined, would be equipped with balloons, and the British would fight back with man-carrying kites; a farfetched conception, perhaps, but it would be more practically demonstrated in two world wars when small English fighter planes took off to fight German bombers.

In the United States a New Hampshire meteorologist convinced Abraham Lincoln of the balloon's efficacy as an observation platform and was authorized to form America's first official air arm. Thus did Thaddeus S. C. Lowe become the first in a long line of frustrated American air leaders. Although his observations had proved valuable during the battles of Fair Oaks and Fredericksburg, Lowe's air force in embryo was disbanded in 1863, two years after it had been formed. The Confederacy launched a single balloon during the War. Constructed from silk dresses donated by Southern belles, its capture by Union soldiers sent out by Lowe, who saw it being raised over Con-

7

A close-up of the Gnome rotary engine which powered the later Blériot aircraft and many of the planes of World War I. This particular engine developed 50-hp and revolved 1,200 times a minute          JARRETT COLLECTION

federate lines, was regarded by Gen. James Longstreet as "one of the meanest tricks of the war." It deprived the South of its last silk dress, the General averred.

But the balloon was not to prove an effective military tool and the regulars of both sides were not disappointed to see it go. A few years later, however, the first airlift in history was to take place during the siege of Paris in the Franco-Prussian war (1870–71). Over a hundred people were evacuated by balloon; from the surrounded French city of the 66 dispatched, 58 landed safely, 6 fell into German hands and 2 were lost without a trace. Thus was the germ of an idea planted. Its exploitation was limited by the crudity of the early craft and the difficulty in controlling and powering them. Innocently, and with determination and energy, the Wrights contributed the final requirements.

Air-minded Europeans, who enjoyed a long tradition of air exploration, adapted the ideas of the Wrights and added innovations of their own—such as wheels, for example, in place of wooden skids for landing gear. France led the way with such pioneers as Gabriel and Henri Voisin, Octave Chanute and Louis Blériot. The latter crossed the English Channel in July 1909—a daring accomplishment, although few at first realized its military implications.

Flying exhibitions became the vogue. Aero clubs proliferated in Britain and France; the airplane became the toy of daring and, often as not, wealthy sportsmen. It was an era of experiment and adventure, an exciting time of "firsts": the first cross-country flight (London to Paris in four hours), the first airmail delivery in 1911 and, in the same year, arrival on the scene of the first lady aeronauts.

One woman flier, Miss Gertrude Bacon, gave voice to the exhilaration of the times when she said, "Picture if you can what it meant for the first time: when all the world of aviation was young and fresh and untried; when to rise at all was a glorious adventure, and to find oneself flying swiftly in the air the too-good-to-be-true realization of a lifelong dream!"

In 1911 a less dreamlike, if more ominous, aspect of aviation was demonstrated in San Francisco when Lt. M. S. Crissy, with P. O. Parmalee as pilot, dropped some small hand-held bombs. By 1912 a crude bombsight was invented and tested; the same year, a machine gun was mounted on a Wright B aircraft and fired. In the Tripolitan War the Italians employed the airplane for military reconnaissance, and during the Balkan War (1912–13) Bulgarian aviators dropped bombs on Turkish positions in Adrianople. The French had recognized the flying machine as an important servant to the traditional infantry and artillery. In April 1912, the Royal Flying Corps had been established in Britain.

The world was on the verge of "a glorious adventure" never dreamed of in the philosophy of Miss Gertrude Bacon.

There were further advances in the realm of flight, during this same period of flitting and sputtering flying machines, in the more venerable airships. Developed out of the difficult-to-control balloons, the airships were proving to be the most practical means of flight. It was in Germany that the most important advances were made with the advent of dirigibles, the rigid airship, under the direction of Count Ferdinand von Zeppelin. The first "zeppelin," as practically all of these craft came to be called, was a 419.8-foot-long giant which was successfully launched on July 2, 1900 at Lake Constance. Almost a decade was devoted by Zeppelin to perfecting his form of airship, and after

A Deperdussin rounding a pylon during a 1913 French air meet; it was a remarkably modern design for the time          FRENCH EMBASSY

several disappointments he confidently launched the first aerial passenger service in 1909. During the period 1911–14, commercial Zeppelins carried more than 10,000 passengers—without a single fatality—over some 107,000 miles. The air filled with winged traffic and obviously a new age had dawned.

The implications of all this ferment and excitement was hinted at by the British aviator Sir Alan Cobham, who, noting Blériot's successful crossing of the English Channel, said, "The day that Blériot flew the Channel marked the end of our insular safety and the beginning of the time when Britain must seek another form of defense besides its ships."

On the eve of the mass devastation that would come to be called the Great War, very few were aware of the full significance of Cobham's prophecy. Included among the innocently ignorant were military and political leaders, even then blundering their countries into war, and two mild bicycle manufacturers from Dayton, Ohio.

# 1914

*The aircraft is all very well for sport—
for the army it is useless.*

—FERDINAND FOCH

The call to arms: notices of mobilization posted in Paris, August 1914

# *When the Imperial German*

Army began its roundabout sweep through Belgium and France on the night of August 4, 1914, its triumphant leaders, disciples of military theorist Karl von Clausewitz, hardly considered the "aeroplane" as essential to their strategic thinking. Their plan of attack, the Schlieffen plan of 1905, had been conceived before aviation had emerged as "a glorious adventure." Besides, wars were won by troops who had taken and occupied specific key cities and ground emplacements—definite territories which could be pointed to on a map. The uncharted air, with its unreal perspectives of the ground, distorting and diminishing, did not figure in the generals' calculations at all.

There were no real military aircraft when the troops began to march in that fateful August. France could boast of a separate Aeronautical Service that could muster about 130 operational planes. The Germans had 230 assorted planes, but all of them were subservient to ground troops and used only for observation and message carrying. In August 1914, the British had barely a hundred planes that could get into the air. None of these aircraft, of whatever nationality, was armed; the airplane as an offensive weapon was unthinkable and it was assigned the role of a flying horse. In Britain, proud though apprehensive cavalrymen complained that the clatter of engines frightened their spirited mounts. They preferred to have nothing to do with the unwieldy, unreliable airplanes. There was fear also, in some quarters, that the noisy, fluttering monsters might supplant the horse-mounted cavalry and thus rob the British army of its single touch of real quality.

Flights over the lines during the early weeks of the war were curiously amiable. Pilots, though on opposing sides, may have been friends in the small select fraternity of the air in prewar years and merely exchanged friendly greetings as they encountered each other in the air. Their respective observers, however, blithely noted troop movements and concentrations on their maps.

It occurred one day to a pilot whose name is now lost to history that his one-time flying friend, now an enemy pilot, was carrying valuable military information. The planes were still not armed, but the fliers affected side arms; after all there was a war on and as participants they should carry weapons. The more bellicose types took to carrying rifles with which to take pot shots at enemy planes, but the vibration of the aircraft, inexperience, and high winds made accuracy impossible. The first aerial gunners undoubtedly put more holes in their own planes than those of the enemy.

Early in the war, French observers were issued bags of bricks in the hope that a lucky pitch might hit a propeller or even a pilot. The idea was modified when an inventive airman tied a brick to the end of a long rope which he then could dangle into the enemy's propeller arc from above. Further refinements included bits of chain (in place of bricks), or rifles crudely mounted at an

13

French troops moving through a Paris suburb to reinforce the left wing, northwest of the city                                   FRENCH EMBASSY

angle on the plane (to miss the propeller), but none of these proved to be as effective as was expected.

To most militarists this kind of warfare was a waste of time which detracted from the primary military function of the airplane—observation. Toward the close of 1914 the German General Staff reported that "experience has shown that a real combat in the air, such as journalists and romancers have described, should be considered a myth. The duty of the aviator is to see, not to fight."

The traditionalists had not, however, reckoned with the youthful aviator, a romancer and adventurer at heart; nor did the traditionalists realize the potential for development possible in the flying machine. To a man, on each side, they clung to their nineteenth-century means of making war.

In August 1914, practically every plane in use by the warring powers was obsolete or obsolescent, it is true. Originally designed for sport, they were hardly to be classed as fighting planes. They were little understood even by those who might have had some idea of their function as war weapons. This was demonstrated, practically, at the beginning by the little Royal Flying Corps, air arm of the British Expeditionary Force. Thirty-seven planes strong, the Corps began moving into France from a field in Dover on August 13,

14

Lt. L. A. Strange, who despite several harrowing aerial adventures survived the war

IMPERIAL WAR MUSEUM, LONDON

1914. Crossing the English Channel, the little force landed near Amiens—the first plane being a B.E.2A piloted by Lt. H. D. Harvey-Kelly of No. 2 Squadron—after almost two hours of flight. The squadrons consisted of a mixed assortment of more-or-less airworthy craft of British and French design—B.E.s, Avros, Blériots and Farmans. It would be a while before it would occur to someone that because of the different performances of these craft, it would be impractical to attempt using them in combined operations. If those planes evidenced little else besides an inclination toward collapsing in a strong wind, their young pilots were characterized by an initiative and daring that would write history.

Among them was Lt. Louis A. Strange, pilot of an Henri Farman in No. 5 Squadron, who reasoned that his craft would better fulfill its mission if fitted with a machine gun. He and his observer (and newly appointed gunner) Lt. L. Penn-Gaskell, mounted a Lewis machine gun on the front of the bathtub-like fuselage. Since their Farman was a pusher-type of aircraft, with the propeller and engine mounted behind the pilot and observer, the machine gun could fire forward without the hazard of the whirling propeller blades within their area of fire. Seated in front of the pilot, in the "bathtub," Penn-Gaskell could man the machine gun.

About a week after they had arrived in France, Strange and Penn-Gaskell

15

# MAURICE FARMAN "LONGHORN" BIPLANE (TYPE 1913).
### (80 H.P. RENAULT.)

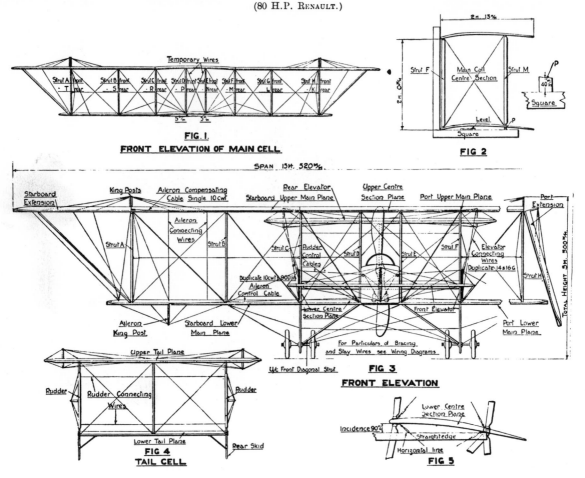

**FIG. I.**
**FRONT ELEVATION OF MAIN CELL**

**FIG 2**

**FIG 3**
**FRONT ELEVATION**

**FIG 4**
**TAIL CELL**

**FIG 5**

Rigging diagram from an R.F.C. manual illustrating the wiring of a Farman Longhorn. The complex system inspired the expression "flying birdcage" for the early planes of World War I, and French mechanics also suggested that in order to check the wiring they merely released a bird inside the wing sections and if it escaped, the wiring had to be repaired         AIR FORCE MUSEUM

were given an opportunity to test their idea. When a German reconnaissance plane was sighted over the Mauberge Aerodrome, the two Britishers dashed to their Farman and took off with their Lewis gun at the ready. A new deadly weapon, they were certain, was about to be born. But they had failed to take into consideration the additional weight of the heavy gun. While the German Rumpler lazily taunted them from an altitude of 5,000 feet, Strange found, to his consternation, that he could not get the Farman much over 3,000 feet in altitude. When he landed the overloaded Farman, Strange was ordered by his commanding officer to remove the Lewis gun from the plane.

Three days later, on August 25, 1914, Lieutenant Harvey-Kelly of No. 2

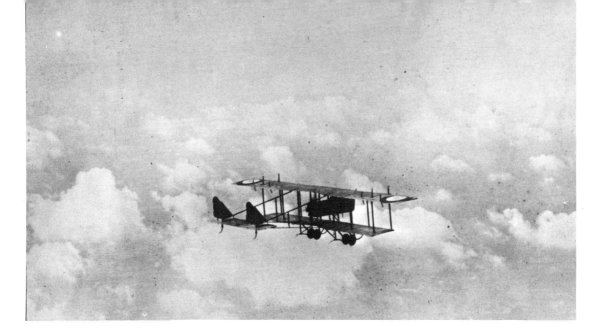

A Farman Shorthorn on a reconnaissance flight over the lines      U. S. Air Force

Squadron, R.F.C., encountered another Rumpler of the type popularly called the Taube (Dove) because of the birdlike appearance of its wing and tail design. It was on this day that Harvey-Kelly introduced another innovation into the air war. While on a flight in company with two other planes of his squadron, Harvey-Kelly sighted a German plane below him on an innocent observation mission. Leading the attack, Harvey-Kelly dived directly at the startled German who, in fear of collision, also dived. Harvey-Kelly remained glued to the tail of the hapless Taube. The other British fliers, quickly catching on to the game, joined in the chase, and before long the surprised and frightened German pilot found himself hemmed in by three British madmen. There was no other course for him but to land his Taube in the most convenient meadow. All the while, incidentally, there were no shots fired for the simple reason that the planes were not armed.

As soon as his Taube had come to a bumpy halt and before the propeller had stopped turning, the frightened German sprinted for a nearby woods. He remained out of sight while Harvey-Kelly, having landed, gave up searching for the German and then set the Taube afire. This was probably the first enemy aircraft brought down by the R. F. C. The fate of the German pilot is unknown, but it is certain that he came away with a new respect for the British.

As for the Taube—it was to become the first celebrated aircraft of the war. It was the conception of an Austrian designer, Josef Etrich, who had failed to interest the German government in his plane but later was able to sell the design to the Rumpler firm. Altogether some twenty aircraft manufacturers produced the Taube; the most successful, however, were those made by Rumpler. About half the planes in use by Germany at the outbreak of the

17

Captured German planes on exhibit in Paris. In the background is an L.V.G. reconnaissance plane. A two-seater Taube is on display in the foreground

war were of this type and the plane became a familiar sight over the Western Front and even over the city of Paris. On August 13, 1914, Lt. Franz von Hiddeson dropped two four-pound bombs from a Taube on the outskirts of the French capital; little damage was done except to French morale.

Taubes appeared regularly over the city to drop leaflets of an exclamatory nature:

PEOPLE OF PARIS! SURRENDER!
*The Germans are at your gates!*
*Tomorrow you will be ours!*

Tradition assigns the delivery of these notes to the famed Max Immelmann who was not yet flying, however, when the leaflets were first dropped. Thus the true identity of the first enterprising aerial propagandist is lost to history. In truth, the leaflets produced no more results than did the first bombs.

From the earliest weeks of the war French airmen had also taken to the idea of carrying bombs, grenades or the fiendish little *flechettes* (bundles of steel darts) to drop upon troops. While these devices proved to be more bothersome than effective, they did not endear the airmen to the ground troops, who almost instinctively fired upon all aircraft, friend or foe. Occasionally a lucky shot hit home, so to speak. More than one British airman suffered wounds more embarrassing than serious while flying over their own ground troops. The incidents led to the introduction of two quite important innovations. Armor was added to the bottom of the pilots' seats (for a time stove lids from British messes disappeared with alarming regularity: these were somehow nailed under the seats). Around the same time it dawned upon someone to paint identifying insignia on the planes as an additional safety precaution. At first only the colorful cockades were used by the British

18

and French; the Germans adopted the Maltese Cross. Later in the war all manner of imaginative personal colorations blossomed along the front. They were the most fancifully decorated aircraft in the history of flight, with performances and pilots to match.

If no one had yet quite fully realized the military possibilities of the airplane, there was definite concern over the Zeppelin's eventual wartime usage. It had, at least, already proved itself as a carrier of men and cargo and was capable of a range that could carry it well beyond the front lines.

With this threat in mind, the Royal Naval Air Service initiated the first bombing mission of the war against the Zeppelin sheds at Dusseldorf. This raid was attempted by two pilots of the R.N.A.S. in tiny Sopwith "Tabloids." One of the best of the early British-designed aircraft, the Tabloid established the superiority of the biplane design as a warplane and boasted, for its time, an impressive performance. It could climb to an altitude of 1,200 feet in just one minute, fly at 92 miles an hour, and remain aloft for almost three hours. First flown in 1913, the Tabloid was the first in an impressive line of Sopwith scout (fighter) planes which included the later more famous "Snipe" and "Camel."

The idea of bombing the Zeppelins in their sheds originated with the First Lord of the Admiralty, Winston Churchill. From the time war had been declared, London had lived in fear of the bombing raids by the great dirigibles which were certain to come. Late in August, Antwerp had been bombed from

A French airdrome from the air. The planes, lower left, are Voisins

The first British aircraft to land in France after the war's outbreak. The ship is a
B.E. 2B of No. 2 Squadron, Royal Flying Corps. The pilot taking his ease at the
base of the haystack is Harvey-Kelly, one of the most intrepid of the early air
fighters                                                                    IMPERIAL WAR MUSEUM, LONDON

a Zeppelin with loss of life and damage to property, including a hospital. In
September, blackout restrictions were instituted by the London Commissioner
of Metropolitan Police to afford some protection from the much expected and
even more feared visits from the dread "Zepps." Although there were no
Zeppelin raids upon London in 1914 (the Germans were neither actually
prepared to carry them out, nor believed that they would be necessary—they
felt that the victorious German army would obviate such measures), the far-
seeing Churchill pressed for strategic employment of the aircraft at his
disposal.

On September 22, four R.N.A.S. planes took off from Antwerp to bomb
Dusseldorf and Cologne. Only one succeeded in reaching a target, and
although the pilot was able to place bombs on one of the sheds, it proved to
be empty. On October 9 the Tabloids of Comdr. Spenser Grey and Flight Lt.
R.L.G. Marix were readied for another attempt at the Zeppelin sheds at
Cologne and Dusseldorf. For most of the morning they were pinned to the
ground by a heavy fog, and spent their time tuning up the planes' quirky
Gnome rotary engines and listening to the shelling of Antwerp. By one o'clock

The Sopwith Tabloid

the fog lifted and the two planes took off. Grey, whose target was at Cologne, found that the sheds were obscured by fog. Unable to locate his primary targets he settled for dropping his bombs on the railroad station in Cologne.

Marix in his Tabloid made the hundred-mile flight to Dusseldorf without incident. Aiming his craft at the huge shed he dived toward it, pulled out at about 600 feet and released the two 20-pound bombs he carried. As he watched, the roof caved in and then in an instant flame and smoke billowed out of the shed. He had caught the new Z-9 in its shed, ignited its hydrogen and totally destroyed the Zeppelin and a machine shop adjacent to the shed; a mechanic who had been on the hangar roof when the bombs fell was killed. Although the Z-9 had been loaded with bombs, they had not been fused and did not detonate.

Watching the havoc he had caused, Marix was pleased, but he quickly found himself under heavy antiaircraft attack. The earlier, unsuccessful raid had alerted the Germans who had set up machine guns and antiaircraft batteries around the shed. The Tabloid was badly mauled by gunfire and Marix

21

The Avro 504A, an outstanding British two-seater biplane

had his hands full coaxing the plane back to friendly lines. He was still twenty miles from his base at Antwerp when the plane began to sputter and he found he had run out of gas. Seeking out a field, he brought the little plane in for a good landing which was observed by a Belgian peasant with a bicycle. Leaving his Tabloid in trust, Marix was able to borrow the two-wheeler and thus transported, returned from the first successful bombing mission of the Great War.

The next mission was more carefully planned. Early in November four new Avro 504s had been sent by ship and train to an airdrome near Belfort from which, it was hoped, the R.N.A.S. would be able to launch an attack on the Zeppelin plant at Friedrichshaven on Lake Constance. Four hours after the aircraft had arrived they were assembled and made ready for the raid. They were powered by 80-hp Gnome engines which were capable of a top speed of 62 miles an hour at 6,500 feet. The long flight to Lake Constance, over the Vosges Mountains and following a carefully charted roundabout route which would not violate Swiss neutrality, would test the Avros' endurance—the planes only could carry just about enough fuel to reach Friedrichshaven and return.

The mission was delayed for a few days while the little force awaited the arrival of two of the pilots who were, it seems, lost en route; bad weather,

22

too, held things up. Because of the cold, the castor oil used as engine lubricant was drained and kept warm. Oil tanks were wrapped in flannel and a close watch was kept on the weather. During a routine test one morning one of the planes was damaged, which postponed the flight again.

Finally on Saturday, November 21, 1914, all elements—men, machines and weather—seemed to be ready (one pilot had been replaced because of illness and an inability to eat or sleep). Around 9:30 the four Avros were lined up and made ready for the historic flight. Although their airframes were factory-fresh, the Gnome engines were not, and after a mere three-minute test were pronounced ready for the long, hazardous mission. The crude bomb release devices were also tested prior to takeoff. Within fifteen minutes the four planes were ready—the first to take off was flown by Squadron Comdr. E. S. Briggs in a/c #873, followed by Flight Comdr. J. F. Babington (#875) and Flight Lt. S. V. Sippe (#874). The fourth Avro developed engine trouble, could not get off the ground, and in addition, in the vain attempt suffered damage to its tail skid. It was decided to ground the plane.

The three airborne Avros, circling the field, continued on the mission so as not to waste fuel. The pilots pointed their craft toward Friedrichshaven. In very loose formation they crossed over the Doubs River and by 10:25 sighted Basle, keeping carefully to the north of the Swiss border over the Black Forest. They continued, at 5,000 feet, over the Rhine Valley with Briggs in the lead. When Schaffhausen (Switzerland) came into view the pilots knew they were approaching Lake Constance and also that they would have to swerve to the north to avoid passing over Swiss territory. About this time Sippe lost sight of Briggs, but could still see Babington about two miles behind.

After about an hour and a half of careful navigation the two planes had arrived at the extreme northwestern end of the lake where, as Sippe noted in his report, he "came down to within 10 feet of water. Continued at this height over lake, passing Constance at a very low altitude, as considered less likelihood of being seen. Crossed lake and hugged north shore until five miles from objective. Started climb and reached 1,200 feet."

Sippe observed antiaircraft bursts near Friedrichshaven, to his left, and assumed the Germans had begun firing upon Briggs. When he was about a half mile from the silvery Zeppelin sheds, Sippe dived down to about 700 feet. Quickly glancing about he could see no other aircraft in the sky; Sippe began his bomb run. He could see hundreds of men lined up along one of the sheds as he began his approach.

"Dropped one bomb in enclosure to put gunners off and," Sippe continued in his report, "when in correct position, two into works and shed. The fourth bomb failed to release." All the while Sippe and his Avro were the targets of machine gun and rifle fire from the ground. Though he made further attempts to release the fourth bomb, Sippe found it impossible. With the shed ablaze, Sippe felt he could start for home with the defective bomb.

His was the only plane to return to Belfort—with barely any fuel in his

Wreckage of a German two-seater observation plane which fell into a forest near
the Western Front                                          CULVER PICTURES

tank and with his Avro shot full of holes; when he landed his right wheel collapsed. Babington had followed Sippe and successfully dropped his bombs
also, leaving a scene of confusion behind him. Flames from a burning shed
had ignited nearby storage tanks, and the explosion shot flames hundreds of
feet into the air, tossing Babington's Avro about. He was also under heavy
ground fire and decided to drop closer to the surface of the lake. He headed
back for France also, finding the field covered with mist. He landed at another field and phoned in the news of his return.

Squadron Commander Briggs remained unaccounted for until the next day
when word was received that he had been shot down, wounded by a soldier
who struck him in the head with a rifle butt, and had been hospitalized as a
prisoner of war.

The Germans were dumbfounded by the attack; they had never expected
so daringly deep a penetration of German territory. Defenses were improved,
security measures were more strictly enforced, and serious thought given to
reorganizing the Zeppelin factory setup. The amount of damage was mini-
mized, but Swiss witnesses reported that in addition to the destruction of a
new Zeppelin, "the factory suffered severe damage."

The air war was accumulating traditions, all of them new. The concept of
the "intrepid" airman, which would be exploited during the late Twenties and
early Thirties in pulp magazines and motion pictures, was beginning to

emerge. Youth and inexperience contributed greatly to this idea, of course, and so did the airman's own feeling of aloofness, of being someone special. If his grounded superiors hardly took him into account in their strategic thinking, neither did the airman give much thought to what it was exactly he was doing in relation to the war that went on below him. His was a private war and, often as not, he was happy to be away from the trenches.

The nature of the air war, detached as it was from muddy earth and moldy traditions, would in a very short time take on highly romantic aspects. The daring adventurers would introduce a form of battle which resembled the jousting of knights as they employed the most modern Twentieth-century weapon according to codes of medieval chivalry. The pilots, most of them barely out of their teens, inhabited a recondite world of their own which, for a time at least, bound them more closely to their enemy than to their own troops on the ground.

Their uniqueness brought them unusual attention; death became a spectacular performance, often before an audience of thousands. One flaming fall from perhaps a mile above the earth somehow seemed much more newsworthy than the death of a hundred infantrymen. The French were the first to realize the news value of their knights of the air and, with the help of willing newsmen, introduced the "ace"—a term, significantly, borrowed from the sporting world—to history. This honorary title was bestowed for the first time upon the prewar aviator Roland Garros, the occasion being the recognition of Garros' victories early in the war. Five planes brought down eventually made a pilot an ace, according to French practice. The Germans, a little more conservative, felt that ten victories would make an airman a *Kanone* (literally, "weapon"). The British maintained a characteristic stiff upper lip and did not accept such grandstanding, feeling—and rightly—that bringing such attention to aerial exploits would affect the morale of ground troops. Unique exploits were, of course, recognized by way of decorations. Many were awarded to airmen. When the United States entered the war, the French ace system was adopted.

No real pattern was discernible during the first few hectic months of the war; practically all of the air exploits were little more than random stunts. Madcap British pilots might force planes down to the ground by crowding them out of the sky, individuals would make daring flights to bomb Zeppelin installations, but the major function of planes remained scouting and reconnaissance.

There were, as early as 1914, foreshadowings of what was to come. One of the first occurred on the Russian front and the hero was Capt. Peter Nesteroff, who had already gained some fame as the first man to loop an airplane. He had also gained notoriety, for his government awarded him with a ten-day prison sentence for subjecting government property—in this case a Nieuport—to "undue risk."

Late in August 1914, Nesteroff took off from his base near the village of Sholkiv (which has since been named for him) in a Morane monoplane.

25

A French Voisin brought down by French antiaircraft fire over Paris. In the early months of the war more planes were lost through accident or by mistake than by enemy action                                                    CULVER PICTURES

Three enemy aircraft, led by the Austrian Baron Rosenthal, had appeared over the field to drop bombs upon it. Nesteroff, whose plane was unarmed like all others of the period, quite simply and deliberately rose to the altitude from which the attackers were dropping bombs and rammed directly into the lead plane. Both he and Rosenthal, with wings locked and burning, plunged to their death. It was Nesteroff's single victory of the war.

The first recorded victory of one aircraft over another which did not entail the destruction of both occurred on October 5, 1914. Engaged in this first air duel were Sgt. Joseph Frantz and his mechanic-gunner Quenault flying in a Viosin biplane from which they attacked two unnamed Germans in a two-seater, described by an eyewitness as an Aviatik (although it was more likely an Albatros, which closely resembled it). Compared to the pusher-type Voisin, the German plane was quite modern in appearance.

A ground observer described this first air battle. "At five minutes past ten there came over the German lines a Voisin biplane. . . . A German machine is at about 1,500 meters. The Frenchman charges straight upon him, holding himself a little above."

There was an exchange of machine-gun fire, for both planes were armed with these weapons, the Voisin with its gun in the front of its fuselage; the

26

Aviatik's mounted in the observer's section of the cockpit. Because he was slightly above, the Frenchman had the advantage. The two planes exchanged sputtering machine-gun fire, although the German was obviously attempting to exploit his plane's superior speed and climbing ability to make a run for home. But then he turned to give the Voisin further battle. The Aviatik was seen to dip three times as if the controls would not respond, then went spinning into the ground.

"We watched this marvelous spectacle from a terrace of the château," the anonymous witness relates. "The Aviatik fell a thousand meters from us in a little wood. We ran toward it. The biplane had plunged into the marshy earth of the woods near a large pond covered with cattails and swamp grass; we went in over our ankles.

"The motor [of the Aviatik] was almost entirely buried in the ground, the fuselage was twisted, and the wings were broken into a thousand pieces. One of the aviators lay quite dead three yards away from the motor. The second, the observer, with beautiful hands exquisitely cared for and perhaps a great Prussian name, was caught under the red motor, now a wreck in flames. He seemed to us to attempt to pull himself out, but the movement was probably convulsive; he looked at us, clawed the earth with his hands, and died before our eyes; help was impossible."

By this time a limousine carrying a general who had witnessed the battle had rushed to the scene of the crash. A few moments later the two Frenchmen appeared—"two young soldiers of twenty years, a sergeant and his mechanic, wearing the caps of aviators. . . . The general embraced them—we pressed their hands. An old woman gathered some flowers in the wood, which she offered to them."

The general Franchet d'Ésperey, promised the two boys proper recognition of their action and, although it took almost a year, Sergeant Frantz was awarded the Cross of the Chevalier of the Legion of Honor and Quenault the *Médaille Militaire*.

As for the Aviatik, "nothing remained but the motor, a bomb which had not exploded, and the twisted fuselage. The two men [having been removed], naked, their clothing entirely burned, lay some meters away, their legs and trunks burned, their arms stiff, only their faces preserved from mutilation."

Their only epitaph seems to have been a comment made by one of the men who had helped to extinguish the fire.

"Boche faces," he said.

A general's embrace, a bouquet gathered by a sweet old lady, the congratulations of older and perhaps wiser men, a twisted wreckage and the scorched bodies of enemy airmen—all of these, too, would become elements in the folklore of the new kind of war. The idea of single combat, plane against plane and man against man, was introduced early and would in the following months come to dominate the aerial war. Meanwhile, the new weapon, employed mainly as an eyes for the infantry, was proving itself most useful. When the British troops lay in the path of General von Kluck's victori-

The "taxis of the Marne," September 6, 1914. When Gen. Michel Maunoury, head of the French Sixth Army confronting Gen. Alexander von Kluck's German First Army, called for reinforcements the French responded in style. To meet the emergency, public conveyances in Paris were taken over; by the next day five infantry battalions (with 800 men in each) were transported by taxi from Paris to the battlefront on the Marne where the German advance was halted

FRENCH EMBASSY

ous army sweeping toward Paris and were in danger of being encircled at Mons, reconnaissance reports from members of the Royal Flying Corps No. 5 Squadron alerted Commander Sir John French of troop concentrations, the movement of supplies and other activity which pointed toward a German attack. Except for scattered ground fire, the Germans paid no serious attention to the British planes flying over their lines. With the information supplied by the R.F.C., French was able to ease out of the Mons salient and order a retreat toward the Marne. To his right, the French Fifth Army had also begun its retreat. That the little British Expeditionary Force had been able to get out with few losses and with all their guns was attributed greatly to the accuracy of the information supplied by Squadrons Number 4 and Number 5, R.F.C. A traditional ground soldier, Sir John French acknowledged the work of the airman in a dispatch: "I wish particularly to bring to your notice the admirable work done by the Royal Flying Corps. Their skill, energy and perserverance have been beyond all praise. They have furnished me with the most complete and accurate information which has been of incalculable value in the conduct of operations."

General Joffre (second from right), with aides, up to view the front after the
Battle of the Marne                                    FRENCH EMBASSY

Another example of air-ground cooperation occurred during the Battle of
the Marne, when British pilots, using radios, assisted in artillery fire direction.

As 1914 drew to a bloody close, the German army had been stopped in
its push toward Paris, having come within twenty-five miles of the city. Opposing armies dug in for a long war of attrition which would be shatteringly
costly as had been foreshadowed at Ypres (October-November, 1914) in
which the British alone lost 50,000 men, killed, wounded or missing. The
six-hundred-mile line of the Western Front was cut into the earth, from the
muddy fields of Flanders to the Swiss border—through the Somme valley,
through Champagne, along the Marne, through Verdun: the war of the
trenches had begun.

In the air, little aircraft were gradually contributing a third dimension to
the so-called "art of war." Some airmen—and some, but fewer, ground men
—were awakening to the airplane's possibilities as an instrument of destruction. The offhand, almost hit-or-miss operations in which the airplane had
engaged began to intimate a future role in the war. The fledglings, having
sprouted more powerful wings, were growing talons.

The Great War settles into the trenches: British and French soldiers in the winter of 1914–15                                    FRENCH EMBASSY

# 1915

*The synchronized machine gun
. . . was an inevitable device.*

—ANTHONY H. G. FOKKER

A Lewis machine gun mounted on the upper wing of a Nieuport. This positioning of the gun enabled the pilot to fire in the direction of flight and over the propeller arc

JARRETT COLLECTION

# *The machine gun*

changed the face of war. The classic concept of troops marching neatly in a straight line toward their objective was shattered by the widespread use of the machine gun, first by the Germans and later by the other fighting powers. A few strategically located machine-gun nests made heroic charging of the ramparts a wasteful act of suicide. Among the early sufferers were the British, whose leaders believed that the function of the infantry was to close with enemy infantry in classic style; consequently, British troops were slaughtered in style.

The machine gun was no sudden innovation, no secret weapon possessed only by the Germans. The French Montigny *mitrailleuse* and the American Gatling (the invention of Richard Jordan Gatling) were early forms of quick-firing weapons. The Gatling, a hand-cranked weapon capable of firing 600 rounds a minute, was used in the American Civil War and in the Spanish-American War. Another American, Hiram Maxim, had developed the first fully automatic machine gun as early as 1889. Resembling a small cannon, the Maxim gun utilized the force of its own recoil to reject empty cartridges and to inject new ones. The early forms of the machine gun were comparatively large and heavy and hardly as mobile as later refinements. In 1911, still another American, Isaac Newton Lewis, produced a lighter form of the weapon which was mounted on the early fighter planes. The drum-fed Lewis gun was easily identified by the round flat ammunition container attached to the top of the barrel. Weighing just a little over 25 pounds, it was much lighter than the regular machine guns which weighed two to three times more. As early as January 1915 the so-called "Baby" Nieuports were equipped with the Lewis gun; it was affixed to the top wing, in order to fire over the propeller, and actuated by a trip-wire which ran from the trigger into the cockpit. This was not an ideal installation for at least two important reasons; the gun was not within reach of the pilot if it developed a stoppage in flight—and jammed guns were anything but a rarity. Also, replacing an empty drum in the air was a feat in itself. The pilot had to stand up in the cockpit, hold the control stick between his knees, remove the empty drum and replace it with a full one—hoping all the while that he would not be attacked by a knightly opponent and that his plane would remain in more or less level flight.

The hazard of this arrangement was given its classic exemplification in the adventure of Lt. Louis Strange in May 1915. This was the same gun-minded young aviator who in August of the previous year had mounted a machine gun in his Farman in a vain attempt to wed machine gun to aircraft. Though his early experiment ended in ignominious failure, Strange was never to lose his obsession—although his experience over the German trenches, at 8,000 feet in the air, might easily have cured him.

Strange was serving with No. 6 Squadron, generally piloting two-seaters on

33

The Martinsyde Scout

reconnaissance missions, until the Squadron acquired a single Martinsyde scout plane. Not only was it a single-seat type of aircraft of rather clean design, it carried a businesslike Lewis machine gun attached to the upper wing. Strange quickly convinced his commanding officer, Maj. Gordon Shepherd, that the plane should be his. Shepherd agreed and Strange graduated from the role of a passenger carrier to a full-fledged fighter pilot.

The Martinsyde was not an ideal aircraft, being slow, not very responsive to controls and not very stable. Strange, who had been flying all types of planes, hardly gave this a thought; the very fact that he was pilot of the obviously formidable "scout" (as fighter planes were then designated) was enough.

Strange was flying over the town of Menin, well inside the German lines and about fifteen miles northeast of Lille, when he spotted a German two-seater, an Aviatik, lazily flying over the front. Strange swooped in for the attack but found that he was unable to match the Aviatik's altitude. The German observer had already begun peppering at him with his machine gun; all Strange was able to do was to lift his plane's nose and pull on the trigger cable. Very soon he had exhausted the entire drum of forty-seven rounds. Releasing his safety belt, Strange stood up in the cockpit to remove the empty drum. As he tugged at the metal container the Martinsyde stalled, flipped over on its back and tossed Strange out of the cockpit. The hapless pilot was

34

over 8,000 feet above the ground, dangling from a spinning, upside-down aircraft with only an ill-fitting Lewis drum to keep him from making the final plunge (needless to say, Strange wore no parachute).

As he would later recall, Strange had been cursing because he had been unable to remove the drum; a moment later he was praying that it would not come off. As the plane continued to spin, Strange managed to get hold of a center section strut—a much more reliable handhold than the ammunition drum—and by some quite energetic kicking and midair chinning finally located the cockpit above him. He hooked a foot into it and then another and pulled himself back into his seat. The plane was still wrong side up and spinning, but Strange skillfully brought it under control. But when he finally righted the plane, he himself dropped into his wicker seat with such force that he went through the bottom, pieces of which became jammed in the controls. Although he was back inside his cockpit, Strange found that he had to clear up the wreckage in the plane before he could bring it under complete control. By this time he was close to the ground; in fact, a German pilot who had observed the incident reported that he had seen an Englishman headed for a crash hanging from an airplane.

Strange leveled out the Martinsyde practically at treetop level and still shaken, returned to his airdrome where he found it difficult to explain to C. O. Shepherd how he had kicked out all the instruments in the plane. In spite of his affinity to exploits of this nature, Louis Strange was to live through the war.

Obviously the machine gun and the fighter plane were made for each other and, although there had been ideas on how these could be effectively brought together, it was not until the spring of 1915 that this was effected. It seemed logical that the most efficient form of armed scout would fire in the direction of flight; thus the pilot would need only to aim the plane at the enemy aircraft and fire. The major problem was the revolving propeller. If the gun, whether rifle or machine gun, were laid along the fuselage in a position where it could be easily aimed by the pilot, it was at the same time in a position to strike the propeller blades. Turning as it did at 1,200 revolutions a minute, it took less than a bullet to shatter the wooden propeller. Guns were therefore stationed atop the wing, as in the case of Strange's Martinsyde, or the French Nieuport; or attached to the fuselage at an angle, or manned over a limited field of fire in the two-seater aircraft. These were not very effective.

Then one day in April 1915, a tiny Morane monoplane appeared in the sky near Épernay to investigate antiaircraft bursts which indicated the presence of enemy observation planes. The faster Morane overtook a two-seater German Albatros, the crew of which barely gave the little plane more than a passing glance. Without an observer, there was no one in the plane to shoot at them so the Germans continued with their reconnaissance. The Morane had now pulled up directly behind the Albatros. The mildly curious Germans peered around to see what the Frenchman was up to, but maintained their planned flight path.

Roland Garros in a prewar photo, when he was a famous barnstorming pilot
FRENCH EMBASSY

Suddenly there was the unmistakable chatter of an automatic weapon; the German pilot, Lt. Hugo Ackner, convulsed and slumped over in the cockpit. The observer, Fritz Dietrichs, stared behind him and saw that little flickers of light appeared directly behind the whirring propeller. It was the last thing he ever saw, for the pilotless Albatros carried him to his death in a wild fall to the earth. The remaining German planes in the flight, having witnessed the strange and deadly incident, fled for home. The shaken survivors in the German two-seaters dived for safety deep inside their lines. When they landed, stricken and ashen-faced, their incredulous squadron mates could not believe that such an aircraft existed. But there was the undeniable proof: one plane and two men had not returned from the patrol.

Panic, carried by rumor, raced through the German airdromes in the sector. If the French had developed a foreward firing gun, the once relatively safe (most fatalities up to that time had resulted from landing accidents or unexplainable air explosions) reconnaissance work would become deadly. But nothing occurred on the front for two weeks after; then on April 15, the same little French Morane shot down an Aviatik. On the 18th yet another Albatros went down in flames. Soon the pilot of the Morane was being hailed in the press as an "ace."

His name was Roland Garros, one of France's most celebrated prewar aviators, an exhibition flier who had won prizes in Europe and America. Son of a successful attorney, Garros had begun to prepare for a career in music

36

when he was attracted to aviation. Instead of developing his piano technique, Garros sought out the great Alberto Santos-Dumont in Paris and under the tutelage of the Brazilian pioneer, learned to fly and began a tour of exhibition flights.

With the coming of war, Garros, like so many other already famous prewar fliers, was assigned to Escadrille M.S. 23. The "M.S." indicated that the squadron flew the Morane-Saulnier monoplane. Among the members of this stellar group were such notables as Armand Pinsard, Adolph Pegoud (the first Frenchman to loop-the-loop), Eugene Gilbert and Marc Pourpe. The last was also a celebrated exhibition flier, only shortly returned from the Far East, where he had picked up a moody, adventurous American mechanic and soldier of fortune by the name of Raoul Lufbery.

The forward-firing machine gun originated in Escadrille M.S. 23, but some question still remains as to the identity of the actual inventor. Eugene Gilbert is supposed to have worked on an idea of firing through the propeller by fastening metal plates to the blades, hoping thus to deflect whatever bullets would happen to strike the blades. One of the reasons given for Gilbert's abandonment of his experiments is that during a test on the ground, two of his friends were killed by ricocheting bullets. In the small community of the French escadrille it is likely that Gilbert and Garros discussed the idea and even collaborated upon it.

The method was anything but efficient. There was always the danger of the deflected rounds doing damage to the plane or pilot. Even more possible (as often happened), even with the metal plates, the propeller would be damaged or knocked out of alignment. The result would be either a splintered propeller or an engine dropping out of the plane. These may well have been additional reasons for Gilbert's abandonment of the project.

Garros, however, persisted and his luck (more than anything) held out. For a period of a little over two weeks he was a terror in the skies until fate caught up with him.

Strangely, the form it took was not the obvious one: his abused and scarred propeller did not shatter—he developed engine trouble on an inconsequential bombing mission to Courtrai. On April 19, 1915, Garros was to attack the rail sidings at that important transportation center. His habit was to approach from an altitude of ten thousand feet, turn off his engine, drop down to a hundred feet over the target and drop his bombs. With a silent engine he undoubtedly hoped to surprise the Germans and the low altitude would permit some degree of accuracy. The problem on the fateful day at Courtrai was that when he tried to switch the Le Rhone engine back to life it would not respond. Garros frantically tried everything he knew but to no avail and had to land behind enemy lines. He did not even have time to burn his Morane completely before they were captured.

Airmen quickly recognized the Morane as the one which had been causing so much trouble in the sector and, of course, they recognized Garros as the

The "Black Knight," Eduard von Schleich, standing before his 1915 Albatros C-I, a two-seater general-purpose aircraft also flown during this period by Oswald Boelcke and Manfred von Richthofen. In 1915 Schleich was not well known, although by 1918 he scored 35 victories over Allied aircraft. He earned his nickname after the death of a close friend in whose memory Schleich had his Albatros painted entirely black. A colorful personality, Schleich once escaped from his hospital room through a window (although weak with dysentery) and took off in his Albatros fighter to engage in combat with some French planes. When he returned from this sortie the medical officers placed guards at the door and window of Schleich's room. Schleich's all-black plane was greatly respected along the French front; it was Schleich, in fact, who shot down the French ace, the beloved René ("Papa") Dorme, in 1917. Schleich survived the war, became an ardent admirer of Adolf Hitler and served as a major general in the *Luftwaffe*

A Fokker E-III equipped with a forward-firing gun. Camouflage has been placed over the white background for the German cross on the wings

great "King of the Air." As was the practice then, he was entertained by his captors before being sent to a prison camp (from which eventually he escaped). But it was his plane which excited most interest. The dread secret was out. Calls between the front and Berlin went out, and arrangements were made to ship what was left of the Morane to Berlin. One more fateful call was made from Berlin to Schwerin, summoning the young Dutch designer Anthony H. G. Fokker to come to the German capital to see the Garros gun. The twenty-five-year-old Fokker, who had been put into business with the help of his wealthy father and friends, had been building planes for the Germans based upon his prewar sports plane. It may be that because of its uncanny resemblance to the captured Morane, the German high command had decided to call in Fokker to study the fixed gun devised by Garros.

Although he was not a trained engineer, and not above adapting the ideas of others to his own use—nor was he overly anxious to share the credit for the accomplishments of his factory with others—Fokker was a brilliant natural mechanical genius and an excellent pilot. He was also an able, if not always practical, executive with a keen instinct for hiring men who would produce the type of plane he wished to manufacture. He was not the actual designer of the famous planes which appeared during the war although he undoubtedly not only had the final say in their development but also may have contributed an idea here and there.

Fokker in later years took full credit for "inventing" the synchronized

39

The British B.E. 2c, often called the Quirk, was an early victim of the German Fokkers equipped with synchronized guns U. S. AIR FORCE

machine gun, but it is likely that he was assisted in this by two of his employees, Luebbe and Leimberger. When he arrived in Berlin, Fokker was shown Garros' plane with its Hotchkiss gun mounted on the fuselage and the propeller with its metal wedges. Fokker was ordered to reproduce the system for German use and to install it on the planes he was building for the German air forces.

"It was a dangerous device for the pilot," Fokker later wrote. "Despite the deflecting wedges, the impact of the bullet might break the propeller, and ricocheting bullets might even strike his own plane." It was clear to Fokker that such a device was not the answer to the problem of the forward-firing machine gun. Nevertheless, it was given to him along with a German Parabellum machine gun and he was ordered to do something within a week. Never having seen a machine gun before, Fokker proceeded to take it apart to study its workings. He then applied himself to the problem at hand. The first thing he did was to discard the Garros idea of metal deflectors on the blades. As he thought the problem through he realized that, in its simplest form, he had to devise a means of not hitting the propeller—of shooting between blades revolving 1,200 times a minute. "This meant that the pilot must not pull the trigger or fire the gun as long as one of the blades was directly in front of the muzzle."

Fokker's solution, and undoubtedly he owed much to Leimberger and Leubbe for it, was to devise a system of gears, cams and levels which synchronized the propeller revolutions and the firing of the gun so that the latter would fire only when the propeller was not in front of the muzzle. The secret

40

was that, rather than attempting to shoot through the propeller arc, the propeller would control the firing of the gun.

Fokker then had the device installed on one of his monoplanes, a prewar type he called the M-5 and which the German army designated the E-I—the "E" for Eindekker (monoplane). Within three days after he had been shown Garros' plane, Fokker, very pleased with himself, arrived back in Berlin driving his sports car with the Eindekker in tow after a drive of over two hundred miles.

When staff officers inspected the plane there was obvious disappointment over the absence of the metal deflectors on the propeller. "In my confidence," Fokker admitted, "I had not figured on the conservative military mind. . . ." For the benefit of the assembled high officers Fokker had the E-I, with tail raised, set up on a target-practice range. The little Oberursel rotary engine was started—this was an 80 hp motor which spun around as fast as the propeller. Fokker then fired three bursts of ten shots each and stopped the engine, and the assembled generals inspected the propeller blades. The consensus was that the arrogant little Dutchman was tricking them in some manner. Obviously, the fact that he had shot in bursts of ten had something to do with it.

Fokker was beginning to seethe by this time and proceeded to fire bursts of a hundred, but still he couldn't satisfy the "conservative military minds." The next objection was that while the gadget seemed to work on the ground, it probably wouldn't work in the air.

"I decided to teach them a lesson which would make them think twice before being skeptical again," Fokker later wrote. He directed that some old airplane wings be placed at one end of the field and then he took off in the Eindekker. Conservative or not, the spectators were curious and had gathered rather closely to the wings—which Fokker knew had been placed over a rocky stretch of ground. From about 900 feet he pointed the nose of the plane toward the wing panels and began firing. The bullets, striking the rocky surfacing beneath the wings, began to whine and ricochet wildly. To his delight, Fokker watched the assembly break up beneath him as even the bravest, most dignified general fled for the safety of nearby hangars.

When he landed, and after the spectators emerged from the hangars, Fokker was happy to show them the wings, which had been chopped up by the bullets. But even that had not been enough—the next demand was that Fokker prove that an enemy plane could be shot down by his gadget. Though he protested, Fokker, a Dutch civilian and not a German, was conveniently transformed into a lieutenant in the German air force, outfitted and sent to the front. According to his own account, though he had the opportunity to fire upon a Farman two-seater, Fokker at just about the moment he was to pull the trigger decided that "the whole job could go to hell." He returned to the field at Douai and informed the Germans of his decision and thus ended his brief military career. The Eindekker with its single forward-firing gun was turned over to a flier by the name of Oswald Boelcke, who would demonstrate its effectiveness.

41

The Fokker Eindekker—E-III—showing the 100-hp Oberursel engine of the rotary type, which revolved with the propeller. A single Spandau machine gun, synchronized to fire through the propeller arc, was mounted on top of the fuselage. The Fokker monoplane was constructed of welded steel tubing, a method of manufacturing which Fokker preferred over all-wood structures. The aircraft, however, was not very strong (despite all the wire bracing) and often succumbed to structural failure                                      JARRETT COLLECTION

A Fokker Eindekker in flight, photographed from the tail of a Quirk it is pursuing. The British plane is slightly visible, upper right    U. S. AIR FORCE

Even after the war Fokker maintained—and possibly actually believed—that he had been the first to invent the synchronized gun for fighter aircraft. He even believed that the Allies did not conceive of such an idea until, one dismal day, a German pilot became lost and landed on a French field by mistake. (For a long time planes carrying the Fokker synchronized guns were forbidden to fly over enemy territory.)

Although Fokker was actually the first to demonstrate the practicality of his synchronized gun, there were several others who had the same idea. He was quite surprised in later years when he was sued by Franz Schneider, who had patented a similar device in July 1913—two years before Fokker had even thought of such a thing. It was not a case of Fokker's borrowing Schneider's idea (although he was hardly above it), but another example of more than one man arriving at the same idea at practically the same time. Schneider too had run up against the military mind, which dismissed his device mainly because it had been conceived by a civilian. Although the Allies were about a year late in producing the synchronized machine gun, it had also been suggested by British inventors, the Edwards brothers, as early as 1914.

43

A treed Quirk, with pilot still in cockpit, waiting for help from below. Accidents such as this—or worse—took more pilots' lives in the early months of the war than actual aerial combat                    U. S. AIR FORCE

This idea was mislaid, misplaced and otherwise lost sight of in the official maze of the War Office.

Even before the Allies were handed Fokker's synchronizing gear by the unfortunate, fog-confused pilot, there were similar devices already in process. Fokker always maintained that it was this mishap that finally gave the Allies a working synchronizing gear; actually the British had installed a Vickers gear on a Bristol Scout in March 1916. It was not until the following month that the first Fokker was captured. In the beginning neither side had such gears in any quantity, not even the Germans. The lag of almost a year was to prove especially costly to the French and English.

Despite the fact that he did not conceive the idea, nor even was the first to invent a gear which made a forward-firing gun on an aircraft possible, Fokker was the first to produce one that actually worked—and all within a few hours.

44

In truth, his device was not completely perfected when it went into use, nor was Fokker's Eindekker a superior aircraft. Still, the period following the introduction of the system devised by Fokker for his little monoplane became popularly called the time of the "Fokker Scourge." The more alliterative term "Fokker Fodder," which would be made popular in later years by writers of pulp aviation fiction, was coined by a Member of Parliament while denouncing the quality of British aircraft as compared to those of the Germans. He was not altogether correct in the coinage or the comparison.

If neither the Fokker synchronization gear nor his E-I was as effective as later they would come to be regarded, the advantage in the war in the air, while not yet fully defined as to its mission and scope, had shifted to Germany. This was the immediate effect of the Fokker device; in its wider meanings, dimly understood at the moment, it would transform the one-time toy into one of the deadliest of weapons.

The very nature of the air war would change once a single man not only flew the plane but also controlled its guns. Random skirmishes and even more random victories were to become the exception. Though it was to come gradually, certainly less dramatically than the term "Fokker Fodder" suggests, the "scout" airplane—the not very reliable eyes of the infantry and field artillery—was giving way to the "pursuit," the airplane of the *chasse* type of French origin, or the fighter. Garros and Fokker, as well as those men who contributed anonymously to the development of the armed single-seat fighter, had cut the ties with the ground and moved the air war into the air. Within months an entirely new form of warfare would stir the imagination of the world.

The period of the Fokker Scourge—roughly from about the late summer of 1915 until the spring of 1916—began when Fokker delivered his Eindekker with its single Parabellum machine gun mounted on the cowling to a popular airman, son of a schoolteacher, Oswald Boelcke. As did most pilots during the early months of the war, Boelcke had gained his flying experience in two-seater observation planes. In April 1915, Boelcke was transferred to Feldfliegerabtielungen 62 (literally "field flying section," consisting of six aircraft; the term was abbreviated to "Fl. Abt." This particular section was assigned the job of photographing and other forms of reconnaissance). By May of 1915 Boelcke was stationed at Douai, France, on the Western Front. It was there that he met and befriended another early colorful German pilot, Max Immelmann.

Though opposites in personality, the two men were equally aggressive in the air. Boelcke was, on the ground at least, mild-mannered, likable and a favorite with his squadron mates; Immelmann was more self-centered, given to arrogance and not popular. However, both shared a keen grasp of the airplane as an offensive weapon of war.

Boelcke was chosen as the first pilot in his squadron to be given the Fokker E-I with the single machine gun; its function within El. Abt. 62 would be to serve as an escort for the less flexible Albatros C-1s used for observation.

45

Members of Feldflieger-Abteilung No. 62 as they were photographed for a German postcard in 1915. In the back row are (left to right) Jon Mulzer, von Schilling, von Cossel, Fromme, von Gusner. In the front row are Salffener, Meding, Oesterreicher, Oswald Boelcke, Fl. Abt. Commander Kastner, Max Immelmann, von Krause and Hess

Compared to the Albatros the Fokker was not a pleasant aircraft to fly—and the added weight of the machine gun did not make it any easier to control. Boelcke engaged his first enemy plane, a French two-seater, while flying the E-I on June 30, 1915, as he was escorting two of his squadron's planes on an observation mission. Boelcke had been flying the Fokker for only a week and was still not completely familiar with its flying characteristics, nor was he completely certain that the machine gun on the cowling would do all the self-assured Fokker had promised. There was an additional concern to consider: he had been given strict orders to keep within the German lines with the Eindekker lest a bit of bad luck deliver the new "secret weapon" into the hands of the enemy.

Boelcke dived toward the French plane, releasing a long burst of fire. The two-seater suddenly turned and appeared to go down in the direction of the French lines. Although the crews of the planes he was escorting claimed that Boelcke had succeeded in shooting down the French plane, it was not seen to crash nor was it officially recognized as the first victory for the Fokker E-I. (Another story is that on August 19 Boelcke attacked a Bristol fighter which also fell behind enemy lines and he was cheated of that credit too.) The probability is that, despite all legends, the first pilot to down an enemy plane with the new Fokker device was Max Immelmann.

In July 1915, attorney-turned-soldier Edmond Thieffry transferred into Belgian air service after a short but adventurous military career. As an ordinary soldier Thieffry was taken prisoner by the Germans within a week after he went into active duty. Escaping on a stolen motorcycle, Thieffry crossed the Dutch border and was promptly interned. Bringing his legal training into action, Thieffry succeeded in talking himself out of internment and was even able to continue on his way in the stolen motorcycle. He then entered the air service and gleaned quite a reputation: he destroyed more Belgian planes than any other Belgian pilot. Thieffry appeared to be accident prone and at first proved himself adept only at wrecking the wrong planes. Afraid to entrust him with the life of an observer, the commanding officers posted Thieffry to a fighter squadron equipped with single-seater Nieuports. Shortly after, Thieffry cracked up his Nieuport and as people ran to the crash, he inadvertently engaged the trigger of the machine gun as he attempted to get out of the wreck and scattered his would-be rescuers under a hail of lead. In time, Thieffry conquered his affinity for accidents and became a dashing air fighter, accounting for ten enemy aircraft. Shot down in February 1918, Thieffry was believed killed but he survived the fall in flames and at the end of the war was Belgium's number three ace. He crashed and died, in 1929, while flying through an African storm                                      JARRETT COLLECTION

Boelcke's first victory, in fact, was shared with his observer-gunner Leutnant von Wuehlisch, who actually shot down a French Morane. It was Boelcke's skill as a pilot as much as von Wuehlisch's as a gunner that resulted in this victory, which some historians claim to be the first air-to-air victory for the Germans (although an earlier one was recorded on May 26, 1915). The definite fall of the Morane occurred on July 6, 1915, after about a half hour of aerial parrying and thrusting. It was the first time Boelcke was involved in a victory. For it von Wuehlisch received the Iron Cross (First Class) and, according to Boelcke's own account, he received "a hearty handshake" (he had already been awarded the Iron Cross for his reconnaissance work earlier in the year).

Immelmann had won his Iron Cross following an encounter with a French plane in which he piloted an unarmed L.V.G. (Luft Verkehers Gesellschaft) B-I two-seater scout. The French plane attacked and Immelmann brought the damaged L.V.G. safely back to his base. This occurred in June 1915. Toward the close of the following month Immelmann, as well as Boelcke, was introduced to the fixed-gun Eindekker. Since there were few such planes available to distribute across the 600-mile Western Front, only one or two were issued to a squadron, generally to the pilot who was regarded as outstanding. Boelcke was therefore presented with the first E-I that came to Fl. Abt. 62.

But nothing had actually been accomplished with the little plane, as has been noted in Boelcke's first attempt at using it as an escort fighter. The first indication of what the plane would do came unexpectedly. The members of Fl. Abt. 62 had overslept, following a drinking-fest the night before, and were awakened on the morning of August 1, 1915 by the sound of bombs falling on their field. A squadron of British B.E. 2cs had appeared, to stage a surprise raid. Scrambling into whatever gear happened to be at hand, the German airmen ran to their planes. Boelcke, one of the last to awaken, found that Immelmann had already taken up one of the Fokkers. Boelcke leaped into the second one and climbed into the sky in search of the British "Quirks," as the B.E.s had come to be called. This plane's extreme stability, and consequent poor maneuverability, made it fairly easy game for the German fighters. But on this particular day, Boelcke was not to score. He pulled up behind the Quirk's tail, and found that his gun jammed without so much as firing a shot. Angry, he hammered away at the Parabellum until he made it worse and, thoroughly disgusted with himself, returned to Douai.

In the meantime one of the B.E.s, which had been pounced on by Immelmann, seemed to be in trouble also. It fluttered about and then went down for a shaky landing upon the field on which only moments before it had been dropping bombs. The rest of the formation, scattered by the attacking Germans in their Fokkers and Albatroses and having dropped their small bomb loads, turned and raced back to their own lines.

When he landed, Immelmann ran over to the grounded B.E. (the initials which originally meant Blériot Experimental, now designated British Experimental). The British pilot, a Lieutenant Reid, was wounded in the arm, the plane's instrument panel was shot to pieces and the engine was heavily damaged. Before turning Reid over as a prisoner of war, the German pilots, with characteristic gallantry, attended to his wounds and made him comfortable. This was a curious exemplification of the brotherhood of airmen, which at times seemed capable of transcending national enmities and which endowed the first air war with some of its unique folklore.

The Fokker fighter plane, with its fixed forward-firing gun, had proved itself. The victory was not an especially impressive one. Because of the load of bombs he carried, Lieutenant Reid had made the raid alone, without an observer-gunner in the plane's other cockpit. Although the B.E. was not a very formidable fighting plane, it is doubtful that Immelmann would have scored so easy a victory had the gunner been along. Just the same, it was the first official victory for the new Fokker device and for it Immelmann was awarded the Iron Cross (First Class), a higher form of recognition then his earlier one.

Although he was not the pilot of legend who dropped the exhortative notes into the streets of Paris, Immelmann soon was to become Germany's first highly touted air hero and known as the *Adler von Lille* ("The Eagle of Lille"). He is also credited with originating the maneuver still called the "Immelmann Turn"—an unexpected reversal of direction made in the middle of a steep climb. As is the case with so many other claims of inventions, other "firsts," accomplishments, and even deaths of the early airmen, the true originator of the "Immelmann Turn" is still a matter of dispute. It is highly likely that the maneuver was used even before the war by the first sportsmen pilots as has been suggested by writers and historians. A more recent objection to crediting Immelmann with the maneuver is that the planes he flew were not capable of executing it. At this late date, it hardly seems terribly important, although more or less recognized authorities seem to agree that Immelmann did employ the particular maneuver in his air fighting.

Likewise, the seriousness of the Fokker Scourge initiated by Immelmann and Boelcke in the E-I with its synchronized gun is questionable. With this plane the Germans did fight at an advantage, but the E-I did not appear in such numbers as to merit the designation of "scourge." Besides the first two stars of the German air services, other pilots—among them Kurt Wintgens, Otto Parschau, G. Leffers and E. von Althaus—also were issued the Eindekker during the winter of 1915–16. Toward the end of 1915 an improved E-II (with a 100 hp Oberursal rotary engine in place of the 80 hp of the E-I) and the even better E-III, with a more powerful engine and twin guns, were produced. Of the former, only 23 were built and the latter numbered no more than 150 (possibly fewer) in April 1916, when the Fokker Scourge was ended with the introduction of better British planes, notably the F.E. 2b and the D.H. 2, and the French Nieuport. The British planes were still in the two-passenger pusher category, but fitted out with as many as four Lewis machine guns (in the case of the F.E.) and a single Lewis (on the D.H. 2). The Nieuport carried a single Hotchkiss (later the Lewis) mounted atop its upper wing which fired over the propeller arc, but while it was not synchronized, like the Eindekker, it could be discharged in the direction of flight by means of the Bowden cable which ran from the gun into the cockpit. This early effective contender with the Fokker monoplanes was the so-called "Bébé" (Baby) Nieuport.

The chief victims of the Fokkers, the so-called Fokker Fodder, were the British B.E.s, which were produced in great quantity even after proved obsolescent. The Quirks were underpowered and, like so many of the early two-seaters, trapped the observer in the forward cockpit from which he could not fire a gun with any efficiency. A single gun was often mounted at an angle (to clear the propeller) on the right side of the fuselage, but it was practically useless. Some Quirks either had a gun mounted on a pillar behind the observer's cockpit (he would then have to fire backwards and over the pilot) or behind the pilot's cockpit, which meant he not only flew the plane but also fired the gun.

If, in retrospect, the Fokker Scourge seems exaggerated now, it was no less real while it was happening to the pilots flying inferior aircraft. The personal influence of Boelcke and Immelmann would prove to be even more significant than the few (relatively) victories they had during the winter of 1915–16. Their philosophy of an offensive air warfare and their advocation of a better system of organization in the fighter units would make a formidable fighting force of the German air arm. Boelcke particularly was influential in evolving a system of tactics—the famous "dicta of Boelcke"—and the eventual formation of the fighting Jagdstaffeln. As an "ace" Boelcke was not only a favorite of the German people, although he did not receive, nor for that matter encourage, the publicity afforded Max Immelmann. He also had the ear of Maj. Hermann von der Lieth-Thomsen, Chief of the German Air Service. Other factors, of course, led to the reorganization of the German air forces (such as the high losses of German aircraft during the Battle of the Somme in 1916), but much of the preliminary doctrine was Boelcke's, which earned him the title of the father of the German fighting forces. The fruit of his efforts would blossom as the famous "Flying Circuses" late in the war, although Boelcke was not destined to live to see them.

Although the Germans had the upper hand during the days of the Fokker Scourge, there was nonetheless no lack of British and French valor, despite inferior equipment. "The Hun enjoys things pretty much his own way," one British pilot wrote late in December 1915. "When will our side get a synchronized gun, too? Then it will be a jolly good even fight all around."

Typical of the spirit of the young British airmen was that exhibited by young Lt. W. B. Rhodes-Moorhouse of No. 2 Squadron, R.F.C., during the second Battle of Ypres in April 1915. Assigned to bomb the critical railroad junction at Courtrai, Rhodes-Moorhouse was the only pilot of the four dispatched to reach the target. Flying solo in a two-seater B.E. 2c, Rhodes-Moorhouse carried, instead of the observer, a hundred-pound bomb. The Allies were in serious trouble on the Western Front: on April 22, 1915, the Germans employed poison gas for the first time. Although, because of the experimental nature of this first gas attack, the Germans had failed to exploit it as much as they might have, they had succeeded in opening a four-mile gap in the vicinity of Ypres, caused over 100,000 Allied casualties and flattened the Ypres salient.

Courtrai, the target of the four Quirks of No. 2 Squadron, lay almost twenty miles east of Ypres. No. 2 Squadron was stationed near Merville— the flight from the airdrome was relatively simple in terms of navigation, a matter of following the La Lys River directly to Courtrai for about forty miles. This was comfortably within the range of the B.E. Despite this, only Rhodes-Moorhouse managed to guide the plane over the target where he released his 100-pounder, which destroyed the station's signal box. Not con-

Lt. W. B. R. Rhodes-Moorhouse

tent with having completed his mission, Rhodes-Moorhouse continued circling over the area, observing German troop activity. To judge from the mass of the concentration, it was fairly obvious that the Germans had intentions of pouring even more troops into the break in the Allied line.

Although it was still too early in the war to have to contend with the Fokkers, the slow-moving Quirk at low altitude was exposed to ground fire. After he had been severely wounded in the left hand, Rhodes-Moorhouse decided it was time to return to Merville with the report of his successful hit and with the intelligence in regard to the large concentration of troops at Courtrai.

Turning about, the young pilot could see the river below him just as he flashed at very low altitude past a church steeple. A sudden burst of machine-gun fire erupted from the belfry and Rhodes-Moorhouse was struck across

The German naval airship L-9, passing over a Zeppelin shed in Germany before setting out to attack England          IMPERIAL WAR MUSEUM, LONDON

the midsection, one slug tearing through his thigh and another through the stomach. Instead of landing for immediate medical attention, Rhodes-Moorhouse continued, in uncertain and befogged flight, back to his base behind the lines. As he explained later, he "didn't want the Germans to get the plane." Nor did he attempt to land at any of the forward positions where he might have obtained early medical attention.

Rhodes-Moorhouse brought the B.E. 2c back to Merville to make a full report of what he had done and seen—and died of his wounds the next day. He was the first British airman to receive the Victoria Cross, Britain's highest award, and equivalent to the American Medal of Honor.

It was in 1915, also, that civilians were first subjected to total war. The long-awaited and dreaded weapon which many believed would bring about the destruction of English and French cities was finally ready to strike. As early as August 6, 1914, the first Zeppelin raid took place—the city of Liège was the target. Hoping to force the Belgians into a quick surrender and in order to break a stiff resistance, it was decided to add the weight of an aerial attack to that of the heavy field artillery concentrations. The thirteen bombs dropped killed nine townspeople and caused some damage, but the first attack by a Zeppelin did not decide the issue. It did, however, set the pattern of what was to come: the killing of noncombatants behind the lines and accomplishing practically nothing of military importance.

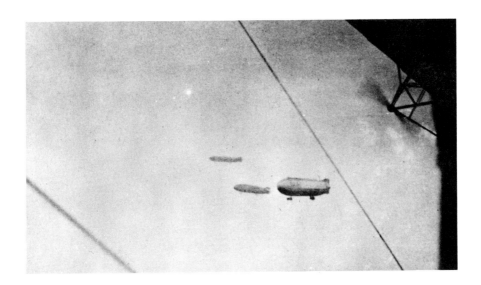

A rare photograph taken of a flight of Zeppelins leaving Germany to bomb England. This was the raid of August 9–10, 1915; the craft are (left to right) the L-10, L-12 and L-13. Photograph was taken by Hans von Schiller, executive officer of the L-11, from which the photograph was taken

LUFTSCHIFFBAU ZEPPELIN, DOUGLAS H. ROBINSON COLLECTION

Meanwhile, the civilian populations, particularly those in England, waited. The German papers predicted fearful carnage and rumors spread of fleets of Zeppelins, numbering as high as fifty, appearing over London to wreak havoc. (Actually, the Germans had only about twenty airships then.) The British were at a loss as to the method to deal with the monsters they were certain would appear. The destruction of the Zeppelins in their sheds as practiced by the Royal Naval Air Service in the latter months of 1914 was one solution, but did not solve the problem of home defense.

But as the end of the year approached, no Zeppelins had yet appeared over England. The Germans had swept into Belgium and from bases set up on the coast, England was within striking distance of aircraft and the longer ranging airship. It was from one of these coastal bases that the first air attack upon England was launched. On December 21, 1914, a single seaplane, piloted by a Lieutenant von Prondzynsk, appeared over Dover and dropped a few bombs, "one of which might have hit a railway station" according to a newspaper report. Actually, all of the bombs dropped harmlessly into the sea. On Christmas Eve another attempt was made, but with little more effect. Even so, the future plans of the German airmen promised parlous days ahead.

While there were advocates in the German high command for terror raids on England, specifically aimed at London, they were kept in check by no less a personage than the Kaiser himself and the Chancellor, Theobold von Beth-mann-Hollweg. London as a target was declared definitely off limits, for both Kaiser and Chancellor hoped for peace with Britain. But there was much bit-

Bombs used in Zeppelin raids. The large 1,000-kg. bomb on the right was called the "Liebesgaben" (love token) for London    JARRETT COLLECTION

ter feeling among the German people for some form of retaliation against the British naval blockade, which not only denied the German war machine critical materials but also pinched the food supply of the ordinary German.

Militarists argued that London itself was a valid military target because it could not be regarded as an open—undefended—city according to the definition of The Hague Convention. Official permission to bomb England was denied until January 9, 1915; even so, London was not to be touched.

Both the German army and navy maintained a force of Zeppelins—the former for battlefield observation and the latter for its fight against the blockade of the Grand Fleet. Chief of the German Naval Airship Division was Kapitan Peter Strasser, whose operational headquarters were at Nordholz, on the North Sea near Cuxhaven. Under his command the naval airships, regarded as "aerial cruisers" by Strasser and a few other imaginative Zeppelin commanders, would take the lead in bringing the war to the British people, thereby "reducing the enemy's will and ability to fight."

Besides having to contend with the delays of officialdom, Strasser also had the equally serious problem of the weather. For all its size, the Zeppelin could operate only in good weather. High winds were especially dangerous and clouds which forced the Zeppelins to descend in order to drop their bombs also exposed them to fire from the ground. In the early weeks of the war the army lost three of its newest Zeppelins in this manner. Daring raids by "crazy" English pilots accounted for two more Zeppelins in their sheds.

54

Strasser began to fear that the entire airship force would be wiped out before it would be able to prove itself. The German defeat at the Marne in September 1914 had brought about reconsideration of bombing England, but because a setback had not entered into the original plan, neither did possible emergency measures. The German army refused to commit its dwindling force of Zeppelins to combined operations with the navy against England, preferring to use the airships for observation and for dropping bombs in cooperation with the ground forces. When a quick victory seemed no longer inevitable, the idea of a London going up in flames, panic among British civilians, the deversion of forces from the Western Front to defend the home islands, began to appear attractive. It was under such pressures that the Kaiser reluctantly authorized the Zeppelin raids upon England.

It took ten days before the weather was favorable for such a raid and on the evening of January 19, 1915 the dreaded Zeppelins struck Britain for the first time. Three navy airships, the L-4, commanded by Magnus von Platen, the L-3, under command of Johann Fritze, and the L-6, captained by Trensch von Buttlar-Brandenfels set out on the mission. Only the first two proceeded to England; the L-6, having developed engine trouble over the North Sea, turned back.

The L-3 and L-4 proceeded with their mission, arriving over the southeastern county of Norfolk. It is doubtful that they knew precisely where they were, for the bombing pattern was erratic. Nine high-explosive bombs were dropped from the L-3 upon Yarmouth (hardly a military target); the L-4 continued inland, dropping high-explosive bombs as it went. Although the radio listening station at Hunstanton was missed, von Platen did considerable damage at King's Lynn and even managed to hit a rail power station. The total casualty list amounted to four killed (two of these women), and seventeen injured (three children). There was some damage, most of it confined to King's Lynn, but in no manner was the first Zeppelin raid upon England spectacular. For their exploit von Platen and Fritze received Iron Crosses along with their pioneer crews. (All were fated to be lost just two months later, when both the L-3 and L-4 went down in a snow storm off the coast of Jutland.)

While neither casualties nor damages were impressive, the reaction in Britain was one of horror and anger. The panic the Germans had hoped to bring about had not materialized; what had, however, was a demand that something be done about protecting England from the Zeppelins. Not once during the raid of the L-3 and L-4 did they come under gunfire either from the ground or in the air. The defenses were, of course, crude and inadequate (for there were not yet any real high-angle guns worth calling antiaircraft weapons); and the primitive planes then available could barely reach the altitude from which the Zeppelins bombed.

The German Naval Airship Division, simultaneously, had its own problems for, early in March, barely a month after the L-3 and L-4 were lost, the L-8 was blown about by a gale over the North Sea. It went floundering around over France, losing altitude, and was ultimately shot down. Shortly after, this ship was replaced by the L-9 commanded by Kapitan Leutnant Mathy, who was destined to blaze an unforgettable name for himself in the history of the military airship.

It was not until May 10 that a raid of any significance was made—and that merely in the form of a prelude. The German army sent out its LZ-38 with Hauptmann Karl Linnarz in command. During the period between the initial raid and while the Germans recovered from their losses to the elements, the English had installed some guns. Taking off from his base in Belgium, Linnarz was headed for London when a heavy concentration of fire from the ground discouraged him and he decided it was better to return. He left behind a message, however:

> You english. We have come and we will come again. Kill or cure. German.

He was a man of his word, however cryptic. Linnarz did return two times, although never getting closer to London than the Thames Estuary. Then on the night of May 31, 1915, the city of London was bombed for the first time. It was the LZ-38 again and Linnarz succeeded in dropping high-explosive and incendiary bombs across a section of the city, leaving a trail of burning wreckage and in it, seven dead and over thirty injured. As before, the attacker returned to his Belgian base unscathed. The German press was triumphant, Linnarz was hailed as a national hero and the German people felt that the English were getting their due for the hunger blockade.

One German paper editorialized:

> At long last the yearned-for retribution has come to the English, a nation of liars and hypocrites . . . the punishment for the uncounted sins of the past. Neither blind hatred nor hot anger inspires our airship heroes, but rather a religious veneration at being chosen as the instruments of Divine wrath.

But the British were not without their instruments of wrath, though for the moment at least they did not claim any heavenly origin for them. The chosen battleground, however, was high in the sky.

On the night of June 6, three army airships, the LZ-37, LZ-38 and the LZ-39, took off from Évère, Belgium to bomb England. On the way, the LZ-38 developed engine trouble and Linnarz returned to the base, where the big ship was placed in its shed. The other two ships, though by now rather confused in a thick mist, continued with their mission.

At almost the same time, several planes of the Royal Naval Air Service, stimulated by the news of the Linnarz attack upon London, were taking off to bomb the sheds at Évère. Arriving over the Zeppelin base around 2 a.m., two Henri Farmans, piloted by Flight Lieutenant J. P. Wilson and Flight Sub-lieutenant J. S. Mills, circled over Évère waiting for the first light of dawn in order to drop their bombs. Because two of the ships were still out, the men on the field did not fire upon the two planes, believing that they were either the airships returning or friendly planes. When a searchlight flashed what must have been a signal into the air, Wilson answered with his flashlight and the two planes circled the shed area for fifteen minutes before they were able to discern the outlines of the great barnlike structures—all the time free of any antiaircraft fire.

Wilson was up at 2,000 feet at 2:20 A.M. when he saw the target area. He dropped his three 65-pound bombs directly into the targets, although not much seemed to happen. Mills followed ten minutes later, to be met by accurate antiaircraft fire; he dived to confuse the aim of the gun crews and then climbed up to 5,000 feet, He dropped his four 20-pound bombs directly into the smoke that curled up from the bombs Wilson had dropped. Suddenly a flash illuminated the entire countryside in a burst of white flame. The LZ-38, first Zeppelin to bomb London, heaved and buckled into a mass of white-hot metal. "Kill or cure," as Linnarz, now a commander temporarily without a ship, had written. The two pilots in their flimsy Farmans had found a cure.

Both Wilson and Mills encountered trouble on their return flights in the form of a thick, white fog. Although neither returned to their base, both managed to land safely.

The same fog, which covered a wide stretch over the North Sea, also caused the two Zeppelins which had headed for England to give up their mission. Even while Wilson and Mills were dropping their bombs upon the base at Évère, another pilot, who had been dispatched to bomb another shed at Berchem St. Agathe, experienced yet another adventure.

He was Flight Sublieutenant Reginald Warneford in a tiny Morane "Parasol." He had taken off from his field at Furnes around 1 A.M.—it was now June 7—carrying six 20-pound bombs, and had been flying for only about five minutes when he was surprised to sight a Zeppelin over Ostend. Electing to give chase to the flying craft instead of continuing on to his scheduled target, Warneford followed. It was a characteristic gesture of the spirit of the early airmen; and of course, to Warneford, a bird more or less in the hand was worth two hidden away in the bush.

It took him three-quarters of an hour, however, to overtake the airship and to get up to an altitude at which he found himself under heavy fire from the Zeppelin. Warneford pulled away to escape the machine-gun fire, hoping to gain height. But the airship turned to pursue him. It was the LZ-37 which had given up trying to find England in the fog and was now attempting to return to Évère.

"At 2:15 A.M. he seemed to stop firing and at 2:25 A.M. I came behind, but well above the Zeppelin," Warneford noted in his post-mission report. "Height then 11,000 feet, and switched off my engine to descend on top of him. When close above him, at 7,000 feet I dropped my bombs, and whilst

Flight Sub-Lieutenant Warneford, who dropped bombs on a German airship and brought it down over Belgium. Warneford was the first airman to accomplish this feat. Awarded the Victoria Cross for his exploit, Warneford died shortly after in a flying accident                    IMPERIAL WAR MUSEUM, LONDON

releasing the last, there was an explosion which lifted my machine and turned it over. The aeroplane was out of control. . . ."

Warneford had released his six bombs as he passed over the LZ-37 at about a height of 150 feet in a flat glide. The force of the great explosion (which could have been caused by a spark of one of his bombs striking metal in the airship rather than by the actual detonation of the bomb) tossed him around, and then both he and the Zeppelin began falling toward the earth. Once he was in a dive, Warneford was able to bring the Morane under control, by which time he could see the ship on the ground "in flames and also that there were pieces of something burning in the air all the way down."

Tragically the metallic inferno crashed down on a convent near Ghent, killing two nuns. One crew member of the LZ-37 survived miraculously, his fall being broken by the roof of the convent. As for Warneford, his Morane developed serious engine trouble as the result of the Zeppelin's explosion. It sputtered and stopped revolving, forcing Warneford to land in enemy territory. He managed to find a small field in the darkness behind a forest near a farmhouse.

Expecting to see German troops at any moment, Warneford at first planned to set the Morane afire. But no one emerged from the nearby farmhouse and no soldiers descended upon him, so he examined his engine and found the gas line had broken; a short piece of it was missing. Warneford was temporarily at a loss until he found his cigarette holder in his pocket and used the end of it to repair the break in the fuel line. This taken care of, he had only to start the rotary engine and make a dash for the cockpit before the Morane got away from him. The popular joke during the war was that a rotary engine was capable of two operating speeds: On and Off. There was no point at which it would idle long enough for the pilot to get to his "office" with any ease.

Warneford worked for over a half hour, miles inside the German lines, using his "torch" (flashlight) and a piece of his cigarette holder to get his Morane back into the air. As he reported with typical understatement, he took off around 3:15 A.M. "after considerable difficulty in starting my engine single-handed." Once airborne, Warneford found himself lost in the fog and finally landed at Cape Gris-Nez instead of his own field. It was not until 10:30 in the morning that Warneford finally arrived back at his own base to learn that he was a national hero. He was the first airman to shoot down a Zeppelin and the second to be awarded the Victoria Cross. (Ten days later Warneford was killed when he and his passenger were thrown out of their cockpits of a new Farman biplane; at this period the planes were not always completely equipped when ready for delivery and Warneford's Farman did not yet have its safety belts installed.)

The loss of the LZ-37 in the air and of the LZ-38 in its shed caused some consternation in German Zeppelin circles. The forward bases in Belgium were abandoned and moved to North Germany. England celebrated the victories of its brave airmen over the hated Hun Zepps. Warneford's exploit particularly demonstrated that the deadly airships could be vanquished in their own element.

On the German side, pressure continued on the part of the German Imperial Navy to heighten the Zeppelin attacks upon London. There was a sentiment in the German high command that effective raids could be accomplished only in mass—squadrons of airships accompanied by bombardment aircraft and escort planes. The suggestion was accompanied by another: that the entire attack be placed under army command. This did not impress the naval airship branch favorably, with Kapitan Peter Strasser, chief of the naval airships, proving especially vocal in his objections to a single command.

Following the disasters in early June, Strasser attempted to step up operations with no real luck. In August the L-12 was lost after being hit by a gun over Dover and fell to the ground in Belgium, where R.N.A.S. planes finished it off with bombs. In mid-August three naval Zeppelins reached England (although not London) and raised the death toll by ten. The army airship service returned to London on September 7, killing eighteen (six of which were children) and injuring thirty-eight.

Clearly the "Zeppelin menace" was not yet over. This was proved when Strasser dispatched three ships to bomb London and another to bomb an

The French Caudron G-III bomber was introduced in 1915 and used through 1917 by both the French and British. Americans used the by then obsolete Caudrons as trainers in 1917–18                                                            FRENCH EMBASSY

iron works at Skinningrove. Leading the strike was the most able of the naval airship commanders, Mathy (in the L-13), accompanied by von Buttlar (in the L-11, and who returned—as was his frequent custom—with engine trouble), Loewe (L-9) and Böcker (L-14; which also developed engine trouble). The army also dispatched the LZ-77, but it failed to find London at all that night.

Mathy's attack occurred on September 8, immediately following the army's raid of the previous night. The ships rose from the scattered bases of North Germany—at Hage, Fuhlsbüttel and Nordholz. It would be a moonless night without too powerful winds and with just a slight cloud cover predicted over London. This last would not interfere with visibility from the gondola of the Zeppelins, but it would make it difficult for the planes of the defense to find them.

The four naval airships were to rendezvous over Helgoland before Loewe was to set his course for the Skinningrove iron works and the other three for London. Leutnant von Buttlar, however, was forced to turn back, which left the L-14 and L-13 to continue with the assigned mission. Böcker in the L-14 was also to develop engine trouble and fail to reach the British capital; Böcker would have to settle for dropping his bombload upon a military training camp and some English countryside in East Dereham. Two soldiers were killed and two civilians and several people injured. But the L-14 never did reach its primary target that night of September 8th.

It was the L-13, with the dedicated, cold Mathy in command, that, as could be expected, reached London. When the restriction was raised on the bombing of London, certain targets such as St. Paul's Cathedral, Westminster Abbey, the Palace, even Parliament among others, were strictly off limits. Following the ever reliable Thames as a guide, Mathy pointed the L-13 toward London; he had no intentions of bombing the off-limits targets, but hoped to erase the Bank of England and smash the bridge at the Tower of London. Nearing the English coast, Mathy was fired upon by the guns of the trawler *Manx Queen* (already alerted by the passage of the L-14); the L-13 climbed out of accurate gun range and continued on its course.

On his way to the city, Mathy dropped his first bombs on the airdrome at Hendon, hoping to eliminate whatever aerial opposition the English might attempt to send out after him. He missed the field, but did hit the suburbs of nearby Golders Green. This was merely a token gesture, for Mathy would be more concerned about the searchlights and the ring of guns around the metropolis.

As he approached inner London, Mathy experienced that chill that comes with discovery—the searchlights began moving across the sky making the slow-moving bulk of the L-13 (it was no less than 536 feet long) an illuminated target for the guns below. Almost immediately the men in the airship could see the flashes below them followed a second later by the crash of the explosion. The ground fire was not at all accurate.

Using the dome of St. Paul's as a navigational checkpoint, Mathy, with characteristic resolution, nosed the ship toward the Bank of England. At approximately 10:45 the first stream of intermixed high explosive and incendiary bombs began falling on the center of London. Without an accurate bombsight the bombs scattered over the city and while, according to his report, Mathy believed he was diretly over his two primary targets, the L-13 never dropped a single bomb on the Bank or the Tower Bridge. For the hated British economic institution Mathy carried a special 660-pound bomb which was dropped into Bartholomew Close, killing two men, a boy, and injuring two women.

Mathy and the L-13 sowed an erratic line of death and fire across the face of London, leaving behind fifteen dead, as many injured, and serious fires. It was the most devastating raid to date. Having completed his mission, and leaving a well-lighted target for the L-14 (which was not to arrive, however), Mathy ordered the L-13 up to 10,000 feet and directed course to be set for the return to Hage. Fortunately, London was spared any further attacks that night. The L-9 completed its mission at Skinningrove, although without creating any great damage and without any casualties.

London had been visited by its first man-made catastrophe and was shaken. The newspapers headlined Mathy's raid as MURDER BY ZEPPELIN, and questions were raised over the absence of aerial protection from the Royal Naval Air Service (actually, the L-9 was pursued by three planes but not overtaken) and a final question: of what use were the guns around the city if they never hit anything and if the citizens were in danger of being hit by shell fragments falling uselessly out of the sky? The London *Times*, however, did make an observation about the people of London stating: "The Zeppelins appear to cause wonderfully little panic at the moment of murder, and no permanent panic afterwards. . . ." If Mathy had not succeeded in pinpointing his targets, he failed even more in what was hoped would be the psychological effect of the Zeppelin. There were no outcries for surrender and peace; instead, there were demands for something to be done and retribution.

Sir Percy Scott, one of the Royal Navy's best gunnery specialists, was placed in charge of the defense of London two days after Mathy's raid. Admiral Scott proposed to strengthen the defenses of the city by increasing and improving its antiaircraft installations. He quickly eliminated the ineffectual pom-pom guns (whose unexploded shells caused more damage to London and Londoners than to the Zeppelins) and began a search for good high-angle guns, which he found in the French 75s. He also, with a foresight unusual in a navy man, suggested that aircraft be stationed around the city. The emphasis however, was, upon a gun defense.

The Royal Flying Corps was brought into the picture, although its total strength, all that could be spared from the Western Front, consisted of only seven B.E. 2c Quirks and one S.E. 4a. Pilots would be on duty to man the planes whenever the alert was given. It was hoped that an alert could be phoned to the pilot in time for him to coax his Quirk to 8,000 feet, from which altitude he might be able to find the German airships. The pilot, provided he had successfully taken off, would patrol in the vicinity of his station for an hour and a half. If he sighted no Zeppelin he would land.

There were hazards involved because of fog and the fact that very little attention had been given to the study of night flight. Takeoffs and landings were perilous and frequently resulted in fatal crashes. If a pilot did succeed in getting into the air, sighting a Zeppelin and maneuvering into a favorable position above the airship, he was then expected to drop bombs upon the German craft through a tube in the floor of the cockpit. A further sense of urgency was added to the preparations when Zeppelins appeared over England on the nights of September 11 and 12th, although neither mission succeeded in reaching London due to unfavorable weather conditions.

On October 13, 1915, however, Strasser dispatched five of his best ships: the L-11, L-13, L-14, L-15 and L-16. Four of them converged on the English coast (the L-11, commanded by von Buttlar, had lagged behind), then steered a course for London. First to arrive was the new L-15 under Leutnant Commander Breithaupt, who began to drop his high explosives and incendiaries, from about 5,000 feet, upon the Strand, London's theatrical district. The time was 9:26 A.M. Although under heavy antiaircraft fire, the L-15 made a bomb run of about fifteen minutes, causing even more damage than had the L-13 the previous month. The casualty toll was at least double and the damage by fire, flying debris and water from broken mains was widespread.

The very heavy fire that met Breithaupt over London discouraged the other Zeppelin commanders from attacking with their customary boldness. The L-16, which was to have accompanied the L-15, became separated, and on seeing the gunfire, Commander Peterson ordered the L-16 to swerve. His

L-12 had gone down when punctured by gunfire two months before and he had been forced to crash-land in Belgium. The sight of the L-15 brightly criss-crossed by shafts of powerful lights and practically bracketed by deadly puffs of explosions was enough to convince Peterson that he must change his plan of attack. Instead he chose to drop his bombs upon a small town of Hertford, to the north of London, where he caused the death of nine civilians (one of them a child) and injured fifteen. Much damage was done to homes, shops and some municipal buildings—although not one was of any military significance.

The great Mathy, in the infamous L-13, also swerved from his course, and apparently uncertain of his position, dropped flares to light up the countryside below him in the hope of seeing a recognizable landmark. He then released a dozen high-explosive bombs upon Guildford; though some damage was done to houses and a break was made in the London and South Western Railway, the only English subject killed was a single swan when bombs fell into the Wey River. Mathy, like Peterson, turned his ship for home. On the way he dropped more bombs upon Woolwich's barracks and arsenal.

Besides breaking a number of windows in the Royal Artillery mess, Mathy also destroyed the dining hall, a stable and a tailor shop. The Woolwich guns continued blasting away with the usual inaccuracy, although somewhere along the line a piece of shrapnel struck one of the L-13's propellers.

The L-14, commanded by Böcker, did not reach London and instead released its bombs over Croydon, hoping to strike a railroad junction there. Instead, the bombs fell into a settled area, damaging homes, killing nine and injuring fifteen. Shortly after, the L-14 and L-13 narrowly missed a midair collision (which Böcker blamed on Mathy).

Now all four airships were headed back to Germany (von Buttlar, in the L-11, only came as far as Norwich before turning back), and London once again rose up in shock and anger. The demands for reprisals were even stronger than after the September raid. Not one of the five planes that took off (often in fog) to search for the airships actually encountered one—and of the five planes, only two succeeded in landing safely after their fruitless flights.

Luckily, once again, there was time for recovery and thinking about the menace of the Zeppelin over England and the Fokker on the Western Front. If the war seemed to shift for a while to the home front, it continued nevertheless to grind away the lives of men on—and over—the Western Front.

But the Zeppelins had finally come and, despite the loss of life and destruction, London had not gone up in smoke. Clearly the people would somehow survive; all that remained was to find some means of dealing with the big airships, to improve the antiaircraft defenses and to bring better aircraft into the battle.

As 1915 drew to an end—the year in which the *Lusitania* had been sunk—the Western Front remained in a bloody deadlock; on the Eastern Front the

Russians had suffered terribly, retreating before the Central Powers as much as three hundred miles.

In the air the war had begun to take on peculiar qualities. Each nation, contrary to all objections to stereotyping, contributed its own style. To oversimplify, the Germans were cautious, systematic and, with the usual exceptions, methodical rather than imaginative. The British were tough, in a gentlemanly way, willing to take the offensive and willing to fight against odds. The French were unpredictable and probably the most responsible for the creation of the concept of the Aces: individualists all, they contributed a certain romantic, albeit perhaps somewhat undisciplined, touch to the war above the trenches. Each, it seemed, chose to go his own way, to fight his own personal war. This was especially true of the pilots of the third branch of the French Flying Service, Aviation de Chasse, which was literally devoted to the chase, the hunt. In the Corps d'Armée, which was primarily devoted to reconnaissance and the bombardment branch, there was less occasion for individual improvisation, but even so, it was not absent.

Capt. Jacques de Sieyès, a veteran of the air wars, minus a leg and two fingers of his right hand, best described the French style when he declared, "Aviation is a game—an amazing game of adventure, of countless thrills, of soul-stirring excitement, a game in which courage, daring, resource, determination, skill, and intelligence achieve honor in life or, if the fates so decree, glory in death."

He summons up the story of one Sergeant de Terline, who "bravely enters combat with five enemy airplanes, and bringing down one, puts the rest to flight. He pursues them, is wounded, his machine gun jammed. In rage, unwilling to let go his prey, he precipitates his more rapid plane into the plane that injured him and drags it in flames with him as he rushes to his death. . . .

"And Captain Erard, an observer who, in directing the firing of the cannons thus to protect the attacks of our infantry, flies so low above the lines that his plane constantly returns riddled with bullets. He ends finally by being hit, and falls, bloody but smiling happily at death, in the midst of the infantrymen whom he has led to victory by sparing their lives."

The air war *à la française* began as an extension of the French sporting scene and, once the idea of "smiling happily at death" came to be accepted, became capriciously deadly. The first German to fall in the war went down under the gun of the Voisin piloted by Joseph Frantz; the first German to die under a forward-firing gun did so when he met the intrepid Roland Garros. Even the ineffectual, though fanciful, idea of throwing bricks at enemy planes was French in origin; as was the rather chilling one of the *flèches,* bundles of steel darts for dropping upon troop concentrations. And the French, too, originated the idea of establishing a squadron composed of its star aerial performers and seeing to it that they received all due attention from the press. One of the most celebrated was originally established on April 1, 1915 as M.S. 3—the M.S. designating that it was outfitted with the Morane-

**CAPITAINE PINSARD**
27 VICTOIRES

At the war's outbreak Armand Pinsard was already serving in Escadrille M.S. 23, in company with such renowned *pilotes* as Roland Garros and Eugène Gilbert. On February 8, 1915, Pinsard had the misfortune of being forced down in enemy territory and imprisoned. Pinsard proved to be a recalcitrant prisoner and devoted much of his energies to devising means of escaping from the various German prisons to which he was sent. Almost a year was spent alternately attempting escape and spending time in solitary confinement until, in March 1916, Pinsard and another prisoner tunneled through a 12-foot wall and escaped. Returning to active duty, Pinsard was forced to familiarize himself with the newer aircraft that had been developed while he was imprisoned, and went on to become France's number eight ace with a total of 27 victories

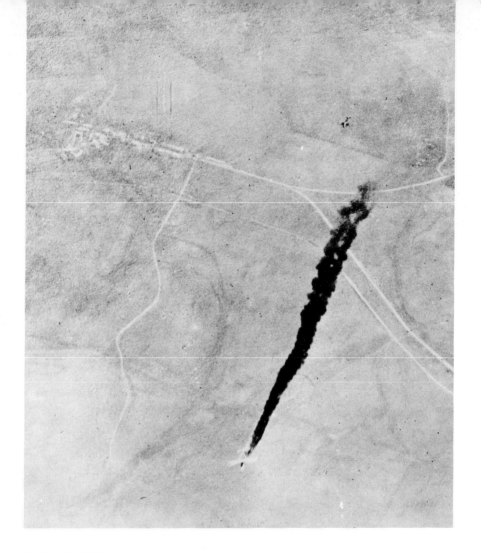

A French Voisin falling in flames after being attacked by a German two-seater, which can be seen slightly above and to the left of the trail of smoke

Saulnier monoplane called the "Bullet"—and popularly called the *Cigognes* ("Storks"). The stylized representation of a stork in flight was its special insignia. In time an entire group of four escadrilles was called "The Storks," but Escadrille No. 3 boasted all of the stars. (Another unit, SPA. 77, formed later, brought together most of France's sports figures; Escadrille M.S. 23 was formed of several of the most famous prewar aviators).

Among the French airmen whose names first became known as early as 1915 were Jean Marie Navarre, who wore a lady's silk stocking instead of a helmet and once took off, expecting to do battle with a Zeppelin, armed with a kitchen knife; and Armand Pinsard, who excited acclaim over his escape after a forced landing behind the German lines. There was Charles Nungesser,

Georges Guynemer poses with his mechanic-observer Jean Guerder (right) after they shot down a German Aviatik on July 19, 1915. "At our last shot," Guynemer recorded in his journal, "the pilot sank down on the fuselage, the observer raised his arms, and the Aviatik fell straight down in flames . . ."

who so frightened the people of Nancy, near which his Escadrille N. 165 was based, that his squadron commander suggested he go and practice such maneuvers over enemy territory. Which Nungesser proceeded to do and for which he was arrested. He was quite regularly in trouble with the authorities, but was destined to live through the war as France's number three ace.

On June 8, 1915, a thin, delicately featured, exquisite young man was posted to Escadrille M.S. 3. The sickly child of an ex-army officer, the twenty-year-old boy, who barely weighed a hundred pounds, had succeeded in getting into the flying service only through the influence of his father. He could not have impressed Capitaine Brocard, commander of M.S. 3, although by July 19 he had succeeded in bringing down his first enemy plane. "A pilot of great spirit and daring," his official citation read, "willing to carry out the most dangerous assignments. After a relentless chase, brought a German airplane to combat, a combat which ended in its crashing in flames." In September, this pilot of "great spirit and daring" was himself shot down while

67

The Nieuport II, the so-called "Bébé," in a nosed-over landing. Installations for LePrieur rockets used in attacking balloons may be seen on the V struts of the wings                    U. S. AIR FORCE

engaging an entire German formation. Crashing in No Man's Land, the pilot was able to return to his unit and by December 24, 1915—his twenty-first birthday—this frail warrior was given the Légion d'Honneur. His delicate features, the eyes dreamlike, reddened slightly as the citation was read:

> During the course of the past two months he has fulfilled two missions of a special nature [flying agents behind the German lines and returning to pick them up] requiring the highest spirit of self-sacrifice, and has engaged in thirteen aerial combats, of which two ended in the destruction in flames of the enemy aircraft.

The delicate pilot, who had just come of age, was the legendary Georges Guynemer whose style of air fighting, which would flower during the following months, was to make him the darling of France. His life was to be brief (even had he survived the war, he would probably have succumbed to tuberculosis) and, in wartime terms, glorious. Characteristically French to the end, Guynemer, according to legend, seemed to vanish—perhaps evaporate would be the better term—in the sky he loved more than life.

It was then, by the close of 1915, that the traditions, the style of air fighting, even the personalities of those men who would be called aces, began to form. For almost a year and a half the high commands of both sides, involved in a war that had not gone according to their various outdated plans, evolved no really effective use of air power. They had enough to think about trying to keep up with what was happening on the ground. Without the guidance of their elders, the young airmen in their rapidly evolving air weapon improvised the first war in the air, a kind of latter-day knight errantry.

With a group of field hands as spectators, more French troops are sent to the Western Front                        FRENCH EMBASSY

# 1916

*Each day brought also a fresh harvest of heroic actions, bloody sacrifices. Each day aviation reaped new honor and new glory.*

—CAPTAIN JACQUES DE SIEYÈS

A view of the Somme sector, showing British caissons and ambulance moving up to the front. Although the Somme offensive was planned before the Germans struck at Verdun, its launching helped to take some of the pressure off the French. Like Verdun, it was a costly battle with little result except slaughter    FRENCH EMBASSY

# It is generally concurred

to the point of cliché, that the advent of the "ace," the lone aerial duelist, introduced "a new breed of man" to a waiting world. If, indeed, they were not actually representatives of a new strain of humanity, they were a new kind of warrior who performed frequently before an audience of thousands and whose deeds were reported in the newspapers all over the world.

That the aces should have received so vast a press coverage in 1916 (and for the duration of the war) is curious in light of the fact that great land armies were engaged that same year in the costly battles of Verdun and the Somme; and the greatest sea battle of the war occurred at Jutland. Casualties literally numbered in the millions, yet the fall of a single ace excited more national mourning. It was simpler emotionally to concentrate on an individual and to become involved with him and his unique way of life—and death —than with the faceless millions who struggled without glamour, and without victory, in the mud.

The German and French high commands learned early to exploit their air heroes, for it gave the people back home something else to think about besides the stalemate on the Western Front, the terrible drain upon the young manhood of their countries, and that the war was simply not going as all the great military minds had hoped it would. The attention given to the warriors of the skies greatly outweighed their strategic contribution; very little was decided in the air during World War I.

Their singular contribution lay more in the province of morale than in the military. This is not to suggest that the generally misused and misunderstood air branches did not have military effect (most of which would not be applied however until one war hence), but the ultimate end was not as great as has been suggested by some historians. It is possible to produce a history of the war in the air and make it appear that it was the only one being fought during 1914–18. But if this were done, there would be no means of concluding it: for, as employed during World War I, air power was not conclusive. Not in the sense that the Combined Bomber Offensive, for all its imperfections, was to help beat Germany, or that the dropping of the atom bomb obviated the necessity of an invasion of Japan during World War II.

The tactical employment of aircraft for observation, photography and for trench strafing and bombardment was limitedly effective in a military sense. But there was not any real overall plan, just as there was no true strategic coordination between the Allies. Consequently, the use of airpower was haphazard and lent itself to the aerial improvisations of the individualists. Alone in the sky in his frail war machine, he could seek out, or avoid, battle as he chose. Formation flying was the exception, not the rule, despite the attempts of the few, such as Britain's Hugh M. Trenchard, who had already begun to visualize the implications of air power.

The Albatros D-I, a single-seater scout which replaced the inferior Fokker Eindekkers. Selected by Boelcke to be used in his Jagdstaffeln, the Albatros proved superior to the British pusher-type planes which had been more than a match for the Fokkers in 1916                    JARRETT COLLECTION

As a possible solution to the Fokker Scourge of late 1915 and early 1916, Trenchard, who was Chief of the Air Staff, and who saw the warplane as "an offensive and not a defensive weapon," stated early in January 1916 that "until the Royal Flying Corps is in possession of a machine as good as, or better than, the German Fokker, it seems that a change in policy and tactics has become necessary. In order to ensure that reconnaissance and photography patrols are allowed a fair chance of success, all fighter aircraft will raid prominent enemy aerodromes and attack any hostile machine that offers combat." In addition, General Trenchard also wrote that "all machines must fly in formations of not less than four units. . ." as a form of self-protection and for better performance. The aerial duel, as he would later declare, Trenchard regarded as "a waste of time and manpower. . . ."

The "new breed of man" was a hunter by nature; he preferred to attack rather than defend, and the most spectacular of them such as Immelmann, Ball and Guynemer were of that singular psychological makeup best described as aggressively daring who, in the phrase of the pulp magazines, "plunged headlong at the foe, with twin guns chattering hate." Some of the aces were neither good pilots nor accurate shots, but men (boys, rather, for many were barely out of their teens) whose technique was simple: you got as close as possible to the enemy, so close that it would be difficult to miss him —and then you shot him down.

In getting this advantage you used all the tricks you could. If the airmen of the Great War were the last exponents of knightly practices, they also practiced some of the knightly methods of dirty fighting. The German fliers, who were mainly on the defensive, rarely crossed their lines, which meant that advantage was theirs. If they were shot down they might be able to land

74

A remarkable World War I aircraft, the Junkers J-2, designed by Dr. Hugo Junkers in 1916. Only six of these planes were built; construction was all-metal, which earned for them the name of "Tin Donkeys." Although not widely used by the German air force, the Junkers were years ahead of their time

and return to battle, provided the landing was more or less a good one. And during the early-morning patrols especially they had yet another advantage: the French and British fliers had the rising sun in their eyes, which made the detection of enemy planes quite difficult. One of the favored tactics, called "the Hun in the sun," was for the German pilots to get up as high as possible and wait for the unwary enemy plane to come by. Unable to gaze into the glare of the sun, the British or French pilot would not see the German until too late. Many a pilot on both sides went down without ever knowing what hit him.

For all the supposed gentlemanly "rules" that came into being, this deception was not regarded as taking unfair advantage, any more than hiding behind trees and rocks on the ground. The more skilled pilots soon learned to exploit their particular field of battle—the sun, clouds, even the wind. The tide of victory frequently fluctuated according to the superiority of the equipment; mastery of the air depended as much upon the planes and guns as the men. Thus did the advantage sway back and forth with the introduction of better planes. The Fokker Eindekker, with its forward-firing synchronized gun, swung the pendulum toward the side of the Germans until mid-1916, when the British D.H. 2, the F.E. 2b and the French Nieuport appeared, to give the Allies the advantage in the air. The Germans countered with the Halberstadt D-II and the Albatros D-I, late in 1916, and once again the

75

Oswald Boelcke (left), in command of Jasta 2, relaxing near the front

Germans ruled the skies over the battlefronts. And so it continued through the war, each contender enjoying supremacy for a short while until the opposing side introduced its latest development. Such improvement was to prove deadly and accelerated the airplane's evolution strikingly.

Even while Trenchard was trying to bring this skittish new former toy—and its even more skittish masters—under some form of tactical control, the Germans, too, were attempting to make something of their air arm. With two such popular heroes as Immelmann and Boelcke—not to mention other lesser gods of the air such as R. Berthold, G. Leffers, Kurt Wintgens—making names for themselves, it was a simple step to begin building what was to become the German air force (*Deutschen Luftstreitkrafte*) around such stars.

In preparation for the battle at Verdun, Boelcke was sent to that sector (called "single-seater fighter command, south"); Immelmann remained in "fighter command, north" opposite the British. The German high command, in selecting the fortress-encircled city of Verdun as their objective, hoped to bring the French out in force to protect it. Their hopes were fully realized, except in victory. The plan was, according to the Chief of the German General Staff, Gen. Erich von Falkenhayn, not to attempt to break through what he believed to be a strongly defended point (although actually it wasn't), but to strike at a sacred point which would bring out all the French *élan* so that "the forces of France will bleed to death." On February 21, 1916, the German barrage by more than 1,200 big guns began, and with it a struggle that would continue for months without any real outcome. Falkenhayn had his

76

Unser erfolgreicher Kampf-Flieger
Leutnant Böhme
502
Postkartenvertrieb W. Sanke
BERLIN N. 37.
Nachdruck wird gerichtlich verfolgt.

Oberleutnant
Immelmann
✝
361
Postkartenvertrieb W. Sanke
BERLIN N. 37.
Nachdruck wird gerichtlich verfolgt.

Hauptmann Boelcke
363
Postkartenvertrieb W. Sanke
BERLIN N. 37.

Hauptmann Buddecke
371
Postkartenvertrieb W. Sanke
BERLIN N. 37.

The Albatros C-III, a two-seater reconnaissance aircraft, was widely used from its introduction in 1916 to the end of the war. Several famed German pilots began their careers flying this plane, among them Manfred von Richthofen, Ernst Udet and Hermann Goering. The Albatros was used as a day bomber as well as for artillery spotting and general reconnaissance                    U. S. AIR FORCE

French blood—but it was heavily tinctured with German blood. (About 350,000 French soldiers died at Verdun and about 300,000 German.)

By the time of the Battle of Verdun, improved British and French planes had begun to appear in France to bring an end to the supremacy of the Fokker. Boelcke would add to his score over Verdun while Immelmann, in the temporarily, and comparatively quiet British sector added to his reputation as the "Eagle of Lille."

While Boelcke was a skillful and courageous pilot, Immelmann was more typical of the ace mentality. Boelcke was scholarly, thoughtful and concerned with passing on his knowledge to others. Immelmann was vain, enjoyed his celebrity and was always eager to add to his score of kills.

Fokker saw to it that the famed Eagle of Lille was supplied with the latest Fokkers, which suited Immelmann although he was to have much trouble with them. With more powerful engines and more firepower he was certain to add to his score. By mid-January, 1916, both Immelmann and Boelcke had accounted for eight official victories each and were simultaneously given the order of the Pour le Merite.

"Those were days I can never forget," Immelmann wrote enthusiastically. "We were invited to dinner with the King of Bavaria, and a couple of days later with the Crown Prince of Bavaria, who gave us the Orders. The King

German pilots await the call to action. In the background are two Albatros D-IIIs, single-seater fighters that helped to bring "Bloody April" to the British Royal Flying Corps. The major differences between the D-III and the D-II was that the former had V struts between the wings. British pilots generally called it the "Vee strutter"                                              JARRETT COLLECTION

of Saxony, the Crown Princes of Prussia and Saxony, Prince Sigismund, the Chief of War Aviation, etc., sent me telegrams of congratulation. They sent them to Boelcke as well. My mail swelled to fifty letters a day. . . ."

Although Immelmann and Boelcke were not the only pilots using the Fokker Eindekkers, a combined total of 16 enemy planes shot down during the period following the introduction of the plane in the summer of 1915 through January 1916 would hardly merit the "Scourge" designation. Yet there were many casualties where once there were very few—and those were caused more frequently by structural or mechanical failure than by enemy action. If the few planes Roland Garros shot down (and more or less official records account for no more than three or four), when he "wreaked havoc all along the western front," caused fear and trembling in the camp of the enemy, so

A later variant of the Albatros observation plane, the C-VII. Powered with a 200-hp Benz engine, in place of the Mercedes of the earlier models, this model was popular with pilots because it was easy to fly. Armament consisted of two machine guns                                                                JARRETT COLLECTION

would the victories of Germany's leading aces. Compared to the victory scores that would come later, their early toll might not seem to deserve the dignity of such a terrible, and impressive, name as "Scourge"—but at the time it was just that.

As fate would have it, neither of these men lived to see the war's end and one—Immelmann—would not actually live long enough to be placed in the top echelons of the German ace tabulations. It may be that he himself succumbed to the Fokker Scourge.

As the improved Eindekkers were introduced, Anthony Fokker saw to it that Germany's star performers received them immediately. Though Boelcke was to find much wrong with them, Immelmann, who was more headlong and uncritical, found them to his liking. Especially so when the E-IV appeared

80

Produced slightly earlier than the D-III, the Albatros D-II was flown by Boelcke and von Richthofen. Boelcke was flying a D-II when he was killed

JARRETT COLLECTION

with twin guns (it was also overpowered by a twin-row, 14-cylinder Oberursal-Gnome engine). One E-IV, made especially for Immelmann, was fitted with three machine guns, the weight of which adversely affected the plane's performance. Immelmann tried this version and then returned to his E-III and the twin Spandau guns.

Immelmann was among the first airmen to employ the Fokker, although it was designed for defense, as an offensive weapon. Taking off on solitary "roving commissions," he developed a method of stalking Allied planes and diving upon them—provided the British or French plane had ventured across the lines—from out of the sun, closing and letting loose a quick burst of machine-gun fire, and then zooming up and away in the "Immelmann Turn."

But the Fokker was not without flaw as a design or invincible as a fighting craft. Nor, in addition, was the Fokker synchronization gear fully perfected. On more than one occasion Immelmann shot himself down by chopping off a blade of his own propeller because the synchronization failed. On May 31, 1916, after he had run his victory total up to 15, Immelmann attacked a small formation of Vickers observation planes. He had pressed the trigger once and his Fokker suddenly tossed into a series of frightening convolutions. The synchronized gear had malfunctioned and Immelmann had shot away half his propeller. Off balance, the engine bucked and tossed in its bed; Immelmann had the presence of mind to switch the ignition off. The gyrations stopped after a few moments, as the engine stopped turning and the pilot could see the shattered propeller. The Eindekker nosed down and plunged toward the ground. Immelmann carefully brought the plane under

81

control and set it down as quickly and gently as possible in the nearest field. On inspecting the damage, he was a little shocked to see that the engine, torn loose from its moorings, had remained in place only because of two frail fittings.

This was naturally accepted as one of the fortunes of war, and soon Immelmann was back over the front with a replacement E-III. For much of early June the so-called Eagle of Lille had been grounded by rainy weather. The Battle of Verdun had reached a climax with the capture of Fort Vaux by the Germans after a bloodily heroic stand by a handful of French *poilus*. Boelcke had already been transferred to the French sector and was germinating his ideas on tactics and organization. Immelmann, who was chosen to form and lead his own fighter unit, remained in the English sector.

On the morning of June 18, in company with three other planes, Immelmann encountered two British F.E. 2bs of the R.F.C. 25th Squadron over Annay, northwest of Douai, inside the German lines. The four German planes pounced on the two-seaters and sent one down burning. They then turned to the remaining F. E. piloted by Lt. George R. McCubbin, whose gunner was a recently transferred ex-infantryman, Corp. J. H. Waller.

The dénouement of the ensuing air battle, typical of so many of that war, has never been resolved. The reader has a choice of three solutions to the mystery of how Max Immelmann died.

The appeerance of the British planes over the lines had activated the German antiaircraft guns in the vicinity. According to one version of the story, these guns continued firing even after the German planes had attacked the British and had signaled by firing a signal flare (which supposedly should have warned the gunners below to stop firing). At the same time, Waller and McCubbin defended themselves with their two Lewis guns. According to this variant of the tale, Waller's gun jammed and McCubbin not only piloted the plane but also manned his own gun.

Then something happened—whether Immelmann's Fokker was struck by the gun of Waller, the gun of McCubbin or by his own antiaircraft fire, can never be ascertained. But the Eindekker began to pitch wildly soon after Immelmann had shot a burst at the F. E. The Fokker climbed convulsively, shuddering and jolting until the after section of the fuselage snapped and the hapless Immelmann plummeted to the ground from about six thousand feet.

The erratic performance of Immelmann's Fokker was observed by one of the other German pilots, Rudolph Heinemann, who wrote of the incident some years after the war. According to Heinemann, the story that was permitted to get out was that Immelmann's death was caused by a structural failure of the plane brought about after he had again shot off his propeller. It remained only for the wild engine to snap the delicate fuselage members near the tail, which fluttered down after the toppling forward section.

Shocked over the loss of Immelmann, whom he believed to be invincible, Heinemann received permission to visit the scene of the crash. Inspecting the Fokker he found that "one propeller blade was practically sawn asunder by

82

The "Fighter Experimental"—F.E. 2B of the British Aircraft Factory, the plane which ended the Fokker Scourge over the Battle of the Somme. The observer sat in the front cockpit and could fire one or two guns from that position (the armament varied); the pilot in the rear cockpit could also fire to the front and rear. Both Max Immelmann and Oswald Boelcke lost their lives in battles with F.E.s (generally called "fees" by their crews)     JARRETT COLLECTION

the shots, that there were the halves of bullet holes along the line of breakage, and that the length of the blade's stump reached exactly to the machine guns' lines of fire. . . ." Once again Immelmann had shot his own propeller to pieces; once again the engine broke away from its support and hung on the upper tubes.

"This time Immelmann was as swift as lightning in cutting off the ignition, but the forward lurch of the engine caused the machine to dip into a nose dive. Immelmann instinctively applied the elevator, but when the machine was pulled up, the engine slid back and aggravated the upward movement. . . ."

Convinced by his inspection that this was how Immelmann had died, Heinemann soon learned, however, that the official version remained unchanged. Fokker, for one, refused to accept the theory that his plane had disintegrated in the air. He, too, insisted upon inspecting the wreckage, and emerged with his theory—that the plane had been struck by German antiaircraft fire (he seems to have overlooked the bullet-riddled propeller). Because the Eindekker resembled the French Morane, it is possible that the German antiaircraft gun crews mistook it for an enemy plane. Thus was the Fokker exonerated, but was to go into a temporary eclipse with the death of its major

83

exponent. The other leading German airman, Boelcke, had already criticized the plane's performance, seemed not very much impressed with Fokker's new "D" series (the single place biplane; "D" designated *Doppeldecker*) and would reveal a preference for the superior Albatros.

Boelcke accepted the theory suggested by Heinemann regarding the death of Immelmann. As far as the German High Command was concerned, the last acceptable explanation for the death of their national hero was that he could have been vanquished by the English so that, while the air battle was mentioned in the newspapers at the time, the more or less official version was that a chance burst of A. A. fire had clipped the wings of the Eagle of Lille. To the twenty-five-year-old Immelmann, who had greatly relished his role as a national celebrity and knight of the air for the Fatherland, it made no difference at all.

His death was cause for national gloom, and steps were taken to protect Germany's other surviving national air hero, Oswald Boelcke. He was not permitted to fly in the Fokker as a precaution, until the unofficial reason for Immelmann's death was determined. In addition, Boelcke was essential to the plans for the formation of a German air force, to the formulation of air tactics, and as a respected and beloved mentor to the younger worshipful pilots. With an eye on the public heart, the German High Command appreciated the wisdom of protecting Boelcke's invincibility also. His ultimate fate was one of the tragic ironies of the war.

Oswald Boelcke was an attractive figure; he seems to have lacked the arrogance that was characteristic of Immelmann, and later, of Richthofen. In the air he may have been as cold a killer as any of them, but on the ground he was warm and likeable. Absolutely dedicated to the cause of the Fatherland, Boelcke did not include French children among its enemies. On one occasion he leaped into a canal to save a French boy who had fallen into the water and could not swim. His "work" would never affect him, although it was the proud boast of one of Boelcke's prize pupils, Richthofen (before he himself became the object of national veneration), that "he eats an Englishman every day before breakfast."

Whatever his personal motivations, whether patriotic or the need to excel (Boelcke was one of six children—the sickly one), Boelcke was a superior air fighter. For all his dash and color, he intellectualized and theorized upon his experiences. His views upon tactics, his technical appraisals of fighter aircraft, and his ideas pertaining to all phases of aerial warfare reveal a keen military mind. Boelcke believed that men and machines could be more effectively employed if they were more intelligently organized according to function.

In Maj. Hermann Lieth-Thomsen, the German Feldflugchef, Boelcke found a sympathetic listener. The conversations he had with his chief and the reports he filed would be Boelcke's legacy to the German air force. His ideas were to be disseminated throughout the entire organization and would prove invaluable to his countrymen and costly to the Allies (in both world wars).

The German losses at Verdun's "barrage line" were convincing proof of ineffectual employment of the two-seaters. The aerial barrage line was raised over the battle area to keep French observation planes from reconnaissance work. The grinding attritional waste below was reflected in the air. Despite the barrage line, French bombers too were getting through to strike at German troops, who raised the cry: "Where are our airmen?" Boelcke did not approve of the tactic of the barrage line and clearly said so. If enemy bombers were to be stopped, it would be only by aggressive units of single-seater fighters which could do it.

By the time of Immelmann's death (June 1916), plans were underway to form a seperate German air force under Gen. Ernst von Hoeppner, whose Chief of Staff would be Major Thomsen. One of the initial steps was to project the formation of single-seater fighter units comprised of 14 aircraft of the "D" (biplane class) into *Jagdstaffeln*. It was hoped that by April 1917 thirty-seven of these *Jasta*s would be organized. These, too, were a portion of Boelcke's legacy, for when combined with superior German planes, and the British inexplicable hesitancy over introducing their new aircraft, that April of 1917 would go down in the history of the R.F.C. as "Bloody April."

Immelmann's death robbed him of the opportunity to lead one of the initially organized *Jastas* already in the forming stages in the summer of 1916. Boelcke had been taken off-combat duty and was sent on a tour of the less glamorous fronts, where he inspired pilots of lesser reputation and also sought out future members of his own *Jasta*. He visited Austria, Turkey, Bulgaria and the Russian front, meeting the other stars and stars to be of the German air force. In Turkey he met the famed *El Schahin* ("The Shooting Hawk"), Hans Buddeke, who would in time command Jasta 4 and on the Russian front he encountered a youthful nobleman, disgruntled in his role as pilot of a two-seater Albatros. The Russian front was too quiet for Manfred von Richthofen, who impressed Boelcke as the type of aggressive pilot for his own forming Jasta 2. (Although the honor of forming the first Jasta was to have fallen to Boelcke, his tour of the Eastern Front took him away from Germany and the Western Front when the first unit was forming; this was Jasta 1, commanded by Hauptmann Martin Zander, which was organized on August 23, 1916.)

Another fine pilot was the somewhat older (for a pilot) Erwin Boehme, who was thirty-seven. As careful as Richthofen (then twenty-four) was headlong, Boehme had much in common with the perceptive Boelcke. Both men whom he chose from the Russian front for his Jasta were destined to play important roles in the life of Oswald Boelcke.

By August, the Battle of the Somme necessitated Boelcke's return to the Western Front, which suited him. He had already made a choice of the elite pilots for his Jasta around which he could build an efficient fighting unit. Besides von Richthofen and Boehme, Boelcke had chosen such pilots as Guenther, Hoehne, Viehweger, Reimann and von Arnim (although the latter was killed before he could report to Jasta 2).

It was at Lagnicourt that the eagles gathered—less than ten miles northeast of Bapaume, close to the Somme front. Both von Richthofen and Reimann reported to Jasta 2 on the same day; only the latter, at the moment, brought anything of value. This was an Albatros D-I, the Jasta's first aircraft. Additional planes, including Fokker biplanes (D-III), were delivered to Lagnicourt but in no great quantities. This was no great handicap, for the judicious Boelcke had no intention of committing his "Cubs," as he referred to them, to combat before they were thoroughly trained. He led them on familiarization flights and in target practice, but only he would venture alone in the vicinity of the lines.

When Boelcke returned from these early-morning patrols the Cubs invariably gathered around him like so many spirited puppies. If their leader's chin was blackened from the smoke of burned powder, they were certain he had "eaten another Englishman before breakfast." And this was generally true, for during the period just prior to the advent of Jasta 2 as a combat unit, Boelcke added to his score of "kills." He was testing his own principles as he taught them to his men. After a battle he would then describe it to his eager pupils, demonstrating his tactics with chalk on a blackboard.

In the middle of September 1916, Jasta 2 had delivery of some Albatros D-IIs, an improvement over the D-I and superior to the Fokker biplanes. On Sunday, September 17, Boelcke led his eager pack over the lines.

The situation over the Somme was critical. The British airmen had taken control of the air, leaving the German ground forces without observation for artillery defense and open to trench strafing from British planes. Commander of the German First Army, General Karl von Bulow, described the effect of British air superiority upon the German ground troops as serious. "Not only did the enemy's airmen direct the artillery fire, undisturbed," he complained, "but by day and night they harassed our infantry with bombs and machine guns in their trenches and shell holes as well as on the march to and from the trenches.

"Although the losses thus caused were comparatively small, their occurrence had an extremely lowering effect on the morale of the troops, who at first were hopeless. The innumerable balloons, hanging like grapes in clusters over the enemy's lines, produced a similar effect, for the troops thought that individual men and machine guns could be picked up and watched by them and subjected to fire under their observation."

Under these conditions the harassed German infantry had adopted a cynical motto: "God punish [the precise German word was *strafe,* which was employed by both sides as a term for the shooting up of ground forces by planes] England, our artillery and our air force." One bitter infantryman who was taken prisoner had written in his diary that "during the day one hardly dares to be seen in the trenches because of the English airplanes. They fly so low that it is a wonder that they do not pull us out of the trenches. Nothing is to be seen of our German hero airmen."

The appearance of Boelcke and his flight of "cubs" over the front on a

A British observation balloon over the lines

beautiful Sunday morning would bring about a change not only in the attitude of the German infantryman but also in the air situation. Leading five eager airmen in a V, Boelcke climbed in order to have the advantage of altitude when they would arrive over the Somme. He quickly spotted two formations of British aircraft, eight B. E. 2cs of No. 12 Squadron on a bombing mission, with an escort of a half dozen F. E. 2bs of No. 11 Squadron providing fighter protection. The target was the railway station at Marcoing.

The British pilots proceeded, apparently unaware of, or indifferent to, the Jasta formation. Boelcke was the first to see the enemy aircraft, for the younger pilots had not yet really acquired the kind of alertness to spot planes quickly. He waggled his wings and climbed higher, his five disciples following. With the sun behind them they could exploit two advantages: the blindness of the British airmen and the ability to dive from above.

Bombs had begun bursting upon the rail center when Boelcke signaled for the attack. As he himself reported the encounter: "With five of my colleagues, I met an enemy squadron of F. E. biplanes returning from the east. From this squadron of eight, six were shot down; only two managed to regain their lines.

"I myself took on the leader and shot holes in his engine so that he was forced to land back of our lines. One of the occupants was slightly wounded. The disabled plane, in approaching the ground, ran full into the cable of a captive balloon, and shortly afterward burst into flames." For Boelcke it was his twenty-seventh victory. Employing the tactics they had all but worship-fully learned at the knee of their master, three other cubs—Boehme, Reimann and Richthofen—also drew blood.

Von Richthofen chose aircraft No. 7018 of No. 11 Squadron, R.F.C., with pilot Lt. L. B. F. Morris and observer-gunner Lt. T. Rees as his quarry. His first attack was not successful and Morris, an experienced pilot, did not present the overeager cub with an easy target. In the rear cockpit Rees manned his Lewis gun in a discouragingly efficient manner. Richthofen dipped his Albatros into a cloud, circled and approached the F. E., which he again mistook for a Vickers. He had succeeded this time in approaching within fifty yards before pressing the levers on the twin Spandaus. From nose to engine Richthofen could see his bullets striking. Pulling up from under the plane, he saw the F. E.'s propeller had stopped turning—and there was no fire coming from Rees' gun position.

His curiosity overcoming caution, Richthofen pulled up alongside the F. E. which, suddenly, dipped and began to fall out of control. Before it could crash, Morris, who had been mortally wounded, revived long enough to pull out of the dive and land the plane in a field. Richthofen had followed the stricken plane down and almost cracked up his own plane landing beside it to see the results of his handiwork.

His stream of fire had struck both Morris and Rees as well as the engine. With the aid of infantrymen who had rushed to the scene, Richthofen removed the two Englishmen from the plane, making them as comfortable as possible (both died before a medical officer could do anything). The man who would come to be known as the "Red Knight of Germany" had made his first kill. Boelcke was so pleased with the performance of his fledglings that he presented them with special mugs at a ceremony in the squadron mess.

Richthofen went Boelcke one better and presented himself with a trophy: a small silver cup upon which he ordered a jeweler in Berlin to inscribe the legend:

*1 Vickers 2 17.9.16*

This was victory number one, mistakenly identified as a Vickers (which the F. E. resembled), carrying two passengers shot down on the 17th of September, 1916. The pattern was established with his first victory; the hunter began to collect his trophies. By the end of 1916 his total would be fifteen. On April 20, 1918, the collection will have grown to eighty. Boelcke was a superb teacher.

Having been successfully blooded, Jasta 2 followed its master on flights over the front. It was on one of these that they witnessed a most unusual occurrence. Boelcke had spotted a British Martinsyde Scout (later to become better known as the "Elephant") of No. 27 Squadron apparently alone. Though it had not proved very effective as a fighter plane, the Martinsyde was fine for reconnaissance and as a bomber. Signaling for the rest of the flight to give him protection from some distant Allied planes, Boelcke dived in for the attack.

As he did, he was pounced upon by another Martinsyde, which had eluded Boelcke's usually careful scanning of the sky. Either it had been inside a cloud or else hidden in the sun. Ignoring the first plane, Boelcke began fencing with the second one; he managed to maneuver into a position to place some bursts into the cockpit. The two adversaries then broke away from each other. In the lull, Boelcke proceeded with his original plan: to attack the plane which was clearly upon an offensive mission (either photographing the lines or, if it carried its 112-pound bomb, on a bombing raid). Intent upon his objective, the pilot of the British plane had not been aware of the exchanges between Boelcke and his own fighter cover and proceeded in level flight.

Boelcke swooped up behind the Martinsyde and, with an economic burst of fire, killed the pilot. The plane crashed to the ground. Quickly he scanned the sky above and around him, saw the other British plane and, pulling back on the control stick, zoomed up to continue the battle.

The Martinsyde pilot made no attempt to maneuver the plane even when Boelcke approached dangerously close. Boelcke pressed the triggers of the Spandaus, saw their punctures appear along the underside of the fuselage; still the pilot took no evasive action. Puzzled, Boelcke pulled up alongside the British plane. It had stopped circling and now pointed toward the British lines. Boelcke was now close enough to read the number on the Martinsyde's vertical stabilizer: 7495. He could also see that Lt. S. Dendrino, the pilot, was dead.

Instead of completing the job, Boelcke waggled his wings and summoned the rest of the flight alongside the Martinsyde. Each man flew close enough to see the dead pilot and the plane which was taking him home. Because he was not afflicted with ace fever, Boelcke could afford to permit the derelict to continue unmolested—in fact, with an honor guard of Germany's most celebrated airmen. When the strange procession reached the lines, the German planes dipped their wings in a chivalrous salute to a brother airman and returned to their own airdrome. Boelcke would remain ever curious as to the fate of that Martinsyde with its strange passenger. He would, of course, never know. Martinsyde No. 7495 continued its flight over the fields of France until its fuel supply was exhausted and came to rest, after a nearly perfect landing, in a meadow behind the British lines. When Dendrino was examined, it was determined that he had been dead too long to have been alive when the plane landed. This was not a unique incident—one other occurred in December 1917 when an R. E. 8 landed with both pilot, Lt. J. L. Sandy, and the observer, Sgt. F. L. Hughes, dead. Both had been dead for more than an hour before the plane had come to earth.

Richthofen, as did many others, both Allied and German, regarded death in the air with a mingling of fear and romanticism. "A glorious death," he called it. "Fight on and fly on to the last drop of blood and fuel—to the last beat of the heart and the last kick of the motor: a death for a knight—a toast for his fellows, friend and foe."

Confronting a knightly death was all part of the game. But it was Boelcke's wish to keep himself and his Jasta members alive. To Boelcke, war was not a game, nor the opportunity for amassing a collection of grisly loving cups. He took no real pleasure from viewing the wreckage of the planes he had shot down; he visited the survivors of his various duels in the hospitals, bringing them gifts. His former enemies respected him and his charges, the members of Jasta 2 practically worshiped him. "I have met about forty men," Richthofen was to recall, "each of whom imagined that he alone had Boelcke's affection. Men whose names were unknown to Boelcke believed that he was particularly fond of them.

"This is a curious phenomenon which I have never noticed in anyone else. Boelcke had not a personal enemy. He was equally pleasant to everybody, making no differences. . . ."

Boelcke's engaging personality, however, in no way interfered with his efficiency as Germany's number one airman. In the period from September 17 through October 28, his score of official "kills" had risen from twenty-seven to forty. Although Boelcke had been shot down twice (each time succeeding in bringing his plane safely down behind the German lines), he was believed to be invincible.

It was on that fateful October 28, 1916, that Boelcke led six Albatros scouts over the lines on a defensive patrol. Following the leader closely were his two prize pupils, Boehme and Richthofen. Inside their lines they saw two British D.H. 2s of No. 24 Squadron. Boelcke indicated that he wanted Richthofen and Boehme to accompany him in the attack on the British pushers, while the three remaining Albatros would provide top cover. In close formation the three planes swooped in. Richthofen suddenly stopped firing when an Albatros came between him and the British D.H. "I looked around and noticed Boelcke settling his victim about two hundred yards away from me," he noted in his diary.

"It was the usual thing. Boelcke would shoot down his opponent and I had to look on. Close to Boelcke flew a good friend of his [Boehme]. It was an interesting struggle. Both men were shooting. It was probable that the Englishman would fall at any moment."

Then Richthofen saw what he could only describe as "an unnatural movement of the two German flying machines." Boehme had accidentally brushed against Boelcke's wing. "Boelcke drew away from his victim and descended in large curves," Richthofen noted. "He did not seem to be falling, but when I saw him descending below me I noticed that part of his plane [wing] had broken off. Now his machine was no longer steerable. It fell accompanied all the time by Boelcke's faithful friend."

As Boelcke vainly attempted to bring his plunging plane under control, the horror-stricken Boehme fluttered around his leader's all-black Albatros like

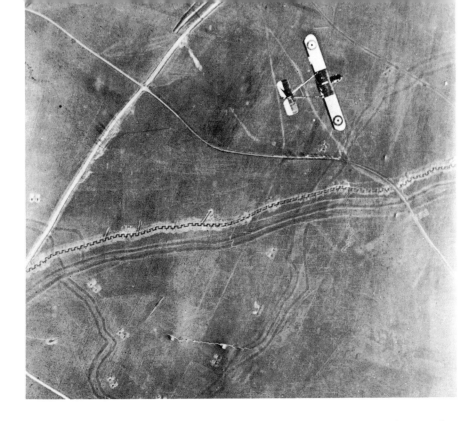

A British F.E. 2B on a reconnaissance flight over the front. Irregular line running through center of the photograph is a trench system. It was while attacking an F.E. that Oswald Boelcke collided with Boehme and fell to his death

U. S. AIR FORCE

an anxious hawk. The spinning plane seemed to come under control momentarily but then struck the earth with tremendous force. In a letter to his mother Richthofen wrote: "His head was smashed by the impact; death was instantaneous." In this same letter he made it clear that, despite their string of victories [he had reached his seventh at the time of Boelcke's death], all was not going their own way. "During six weeks," he told his mother, "we have had out of twelve pilots six dead and one wounded, while two have suffered a complete nervous collapse." This, however, was the unromantic aspect of their jousting in the skies and Richthofen assured his mother, "The ill luck of all the others has not yet affected my nerves."

Boehme, though absolved of any blame in the accidental death of Boelcke, was inconsolable. Of all those who claimed an intimacy with Boelcke, he was the single one who, according to Richthofen, could honestly be called their leader's best friend. He talked of suicide, but was dissuaded from that and in time became the commander of Jasta 2 which was renamed, by Imperial Decree, Jasta Boelcke.

If the death of Immelmann had had deep effect, Boelcke's was even deeper. "During the funeral services," Richthofen wrote, "and in the procession, I carried a pillow displaying his decorations. The funeral was like that of a

91

reigning prince." Even the British responded to his death. Flying high over Cambrai they dropped wreaths bearing such inscriptions as:

*To the memory of Captain Boelcke, our brave and chivalrous opponent. From the English Royal Flying Corps.*

One note even bore an apology for tardiness, explaining that the "weather has prevented us from sending it earlier. We mourn with his relatives and friends. We all recognize his bravery." From a nearby prison camp came yet another wreath with the message: "To a much admired and honored enemy from the British officers who are prisoners of war. . . ."

A special funeral train later bore the body of Boelcke to Germany where he was buried, deeply mourned as the leading airman of the German air force. The kindly and yet efficiently deadly twenty-five-year-old Boelcke had left behind him a legend and a legacy of death. His cubs would continue with his principles of air fighting. His favorite, Boehme, would accumulate two dozen victories before he fell in combat in 1917. His second favorite, Richthofen, would make an even greater name for himself than Boelcke had.

The French had not sent any wreaths upon the death of the great Boelcke. He had appeared over Verdun during the opening of that battle where he soon increased his score. But in time, numerical superiority and the French madcap approach to aerial warfare wrested control of the air over Verdun from the Germans. Boelcke had complained about an unusual switch in the French tactic. "They were sending out as many as twelve fighters to protect two observation machines," he wrote. "It was seldom that we could get through this protecting screen to reach the observation aircraft."

Such effective formation efforts, however, were not the rule but rather the exception of the French individualism. Typical of the French pilot was Jean Navarre, son of a wealthy manufacturer, who claimed to hate killing. He loved flying and often entertained the front-line troops with acrobatics in his all-red Morane when he could find no enemy planes to attack. Frequently under arrest for military misdemeanors, Navarre refused to comply with military discipline, keep an official logbook, or submit to the emerging concept of tactics. He quickly attracted attention during the early phase of the war by forcing down a German Aviatik two-seater—the third official French victory of the war. This was accomplished in a two-seater Morane and, Navarre found the single-seat Morane "Bullet" more suitable to his temperament. It was while serving with Escadrille N. 67, flying the Nieuport, that Navarre was to take part in more than 250 combats over Verdun, and by May 19, 1916, had brought down twelve German planes.

Navarre was a handsome figure—his sensual mouth and heavy-lidded eyes made him a favorite in Paris, where he rarely failed to shock the authorities with his so-called "convalescent" leaves. With his collar up and wearing his trademark, a lady's silk stocking as a cap, he was a romantically dashing, if un-

Jean Marie Navarre, the erratic French ace, standing before his plane, a Morane-Saulnier Parasol. Severe wounds and the death of his brother were to affect Navarre's mental stability. He once chased gendarmes in Paris along the sidewalk in his car. Navarre died attempting to fly a plane through the Arc de Triomphe less than a year after the war ended

disciplined, representative of the French flier. Severely wounded in an air battle in June 1916, Navarre was forced to spend practically all of the remainder of the war in the hospital, where he displayed a violent temper. The death of his brother not long after he had been hospitalized affected him so deeply that Navarre required treatment in a mental institution. He lived through the war but died in an attempt to fly through the Arc de Triomphe in 1919.

Charles Nungesser was another French individualist; as dashing as Navarre but apparently indestructible (he, too, was to live through the war only to die in a peacetime aircraft). As a restless youth, Nungesser had exhibited an early liking for sports, among them boxing and racing. He had even taken off in a plane without previous instruction, actually flying it and bringing it down to a not very neat landing—but he had flown. He even considered, shortly after, the design of his own aircraft but was interrupted by the outbreak of the war.

Charles Nungesser, called "The Indestructible" because of the many wounds and crashes he survived. In 1916 he spent two months in the hospital after a severe crash; but in 1916 he also scored twenty-one victories over German aircraft. The skull-and-crossbones insignia on the side of his plane was Nungesser's private trademark                                                         JARRETT COLLECTION

Nungesser's first military service was with the 2nd Hussars in which he distinguished himself, during the retreat to the Marne, by capturing a German staff car (after killing all the occupants). In company with two French infantrymen, Nungesser then dashed to the French lines under fire by both sides: the French shooting at the German car and the Germans at the three Frenchmen in the car. The exploit won Nungesser the *Medaille Militaire,* and permission to keep the German car he had captured. Nungesser then requested and received a transfer to the Air Service.

Reporting in at Avord, the French training school, in January 1915, Nungesser began his aerial career in Farmans; on receiving his brevet, he was sent to Saint-Pol, near Dunkirk, where he was to serve as a pilot in the Escadrille V. B. 106. The Voisin he flew was used in reconnaissance, which did not please Nungesser, who had repeatedly requested duty with the "fighters."

He had been with his unit for barely a month when he was shot down ignominiously by antiaircraft fire. Worse, he had been enticed into range of the A. A. guns by an Albatros which had refused to fight. Swearing vengeance, Nungesser continued in his attempts to use the clumsy Voisin as an offensive fighter plane.

Then on July 31, 1915, after completing reconnaissance and bombing missions, Nungesser caught an Albatros two-seater over the lines. Deftly manuevering the Voisin into position, he ordered his observer to open fire upon the German plane. Some return fire came from the Albatros but neither Nungesser nor his gunner-observer was hit. Another exchange disabled the engine of the Albatros, which attempted to glide back over into the German lines. With a sure hand and an inflamed temper, Nungesser ran interference and forced the German plane to land in Allied territory.

Obviously such a pilot was not to be wasted upon mundane operations; in November 1915, Nungesser was transferred to Escadrille N. 65. Happily, Nungesser found the little Nieuport a fine mount and ordered his private insignia—a skull and crossed bones—painted upon the plane. It would not be a popular marking, as far as the Germans were concerned, during 1916. The year opened inauspiciously for Nungesser, who spun into the ground while testing a new biplane fighter on January 29. Among his lesser injuries were two broken legs. It seemed that the flying career of Nungesser was finished, but even before he had fully recovered, the French flier hobbled on his crutches to a Nieuport, was lifted into the cockpit and dazzled an admiring crowd with his acrobatics.

As soon as he was back with Escadrille N. 65, Nungesser proceeded to add to his score of enemy aircraft and to his own scars. He was wounded no less than seventeen times in battle and crash landings. He walked with a cane, had his jaw wired because of multiple injuries, and his smile revealed a double row of gold teeth (he had lost his own when a control stick perforated his palate). He was regularly in and out of the hospital throughout the war and just as consistently refused the medical discharge to which he was entitled.

By the close of 1916 Nungesser had accounted for twenty-one enemy aircraft (this score included balloons also). He was an aggressive, headlong fighter, typically French and one of the prototypes of the fighter pilot. On September 26 of that year, Nungesser took off, on a bet with his mechanic Pochon, and burned a German plane and observation balloon before 8 A.M. In the afternoon he went to the aid of a British plane, around which a half dozen German planes had swarmed, and drove them off, one falling a victim to his guns and crashing near the British sector.

Following his twenty-first victory, Nungesser was readmitted to the hospital, where he had his badly set fractures reset and spent many months, under some protest, resting. Even so, he accepted this with the concession that as soon as he felt he was able, he would be granted a roving commission. Toward this end he was even presented with a special Nieuport, powered with a

A Nieuport 17 in flight. Of French design, this plane was also used by the British. The favorite plane of Albert Ball, it was also flown by William Bishop. The Nieuport at this time was armed with a single Lewis machine gun mounted on the top wing to fire over the propeller. Its only unfortunate quality was that it was structurally weak and tended to shed its upper wing in a dive. The famed Stork Squadron (the *Cigognes*) flew this plane during 1916 until the Spad supplanted it

U. S. AIR FORCE

Clerget engine. It would not be until the spring of 1917 that Nungesser would feel sufficiently mended to go back into action. The battered young man then more than doubled his score.

The physical opposite of Nungesser was frail George Guynemer, who appeared at Avord for flight training in March of 1915, just a few days after Nungesser had left. The frequently rejected Guynemer, son of an ex-army officer, was anything but a military type. He looked more like a poet than France's number one war hero. Lacking the physical equipment, Guynemer enveloped himself in the world's newest weapon and invested it with his own fervor and nervous courage. Not a true tactician, Guynemer—although he meticulously checked his weapons, ammunition and aircraft before taking off —fought impetuously and was a superb marksman. He simply plunged at his enemy and shot it out. Such tactics, or rather lack of them, often as not disconcerted the enemy pilot, threw off his aim and gave Guynemer the momentary advantage.

It did not always work, however, and Guynemer was shot down seven times during his remarkable career. It began officially on June 8, 1915, when Guynemer was assigned to Escadrille M.S. 3; on July 19, he burned his first

Insignia of the Lafayette Escadrille designed by Edward F. Hinkle, who adopted the trademark of the Savage Arms Manufacturing Company. The war-whooping Indian appeared on the boxes in which ammunition was shipped to the fighting units. Hinkle decided to use a Sioux Indian instead of the Seminole used by Savage

German aircraft. In September he was shot down himself, for the first time; Guynemer crashed in No Man's Land and was rescued by French infantry troops, who, according to legend, staged a charge to assure Guynemer a reasonably safe place to land.

During the Battle of Verdun, Guynemer's victory tabulation grew as he flew sortie after sortie. "His passion for combat fairly devoured him," one devoted writer observed. Frequently he returned from these combats with his plane shot to ribbons. In company with such *pilotes* as De LaTour, Deullin, Dorme and Heurtaux, Guynemer made the air over Verdun lethal for German aircraft. By the close of 1916, Guynemer, just twenty-one, had destroyed twenty-five enemy aircraft and was the darling of the French people.

So were a brash young company of men who had been organized as Escadrille N. 124, more popularly called the *Escadrille Américaine,* on April 17, 1916. They were seven young Americans who, for assorted reasons, had chosen to fight for France. Most of them were scions of wealthy families; one was a soldier of fortune. Because of official complaints lodged in Washington by the German Embassy, which claimed the name of the squadron was a violation of American neutrality, the little band came to be called the Lafayette Escadrille.

The idea for an all-American, volunteer squadron probably originated with Norman Prince, originally of Prides Crossing, Massachusetts, graduate

97

of Harvard Law School and, at the time of the war's outbreak, a practicing Chicago attorney. Closely associated with him in the early talking stage of the *Escadrille Américane* was William Thaw, a wealthy "sportsman" from Pittsburgh. Both men had learned to fly at their own expense before the war. Early in the war both had gone to France to enlist in the armed forces; Thaw who was actually in France when the war began, became a member of the French Foreign Legion (which required no oath of allegiance and therefore did not jeopordize his American citizenship); he served for a time with the infantry.

Prince, like so many other Americans, set out for France specifically to fight the Hun. He immediately entered the Air Service and in May 1915 was assigned to Escadrille V.B. 108. Piloting the early Viosins, Prince participated in many "bomb-dropping" raids. All the while, he thought and talked about bringing all the Americans scattered through the Foreign Legion, ambulance service and the Air Service together into a single flying unit.

In the meantime, William Thaw had transferred from the Legion, after some front-line service, into the French aviation. So had James Bach, a son of wealth and an American citizen though French born, and Bert Hall, the one mysterious member of the Lafayette—an American of Southern birth and a professional soldier of fortune. Thaw was sent to a bombing squadron and Bach and Hall to Pau, where they learned to fly the little Nieuports.

Prince's idea had come to the attention of Dr. Edmund Gros in the spring of 1915. An American who practiced in Paris, Dr. Gros was one of the key figures in the forming of the American Ambulance Service. The good doctor seems to have arrived at the same idea as had Prince, for in recollecting, later in the war, how the Lafayette Escadrille had come into being, he said that he "was dreaming of a *squadrilla* of American volunteers who would express their sympathy for France in a material form. I believed that these boys were to be but the vanguard of other great hosts that would come from America some day."

While the "dream" was forming, other Americans had been coming to France "to express their sympathy for France in a material form." Among them were the brooding Victor Chapman, son of John Jay Chapman, who had been caught in France by the outbreak of the war while a student of architecture, and Kiffin Rockwell, graduate of the University of Virginia, who sailed for France when the war had barely begun. Both Chapman and Rockwell, would express their sympathy for France with their lives—neither would survive the war. But both became folk heroes in the eyes of the French.

Forming the American squadron was not a simple job. Because of America's neutrality, there were international complications and the French had their hands full with other problems. So the indefatigable Dr. Gros worked upon his friends, held meetings, eventually formed a committee and began an active fund-raising campaign. In order to volunteer for France the Americans had to find devious means of enlisting (in order to retain their citizenship). It was then necessary, in Gros' phrase, to "obtain the necessary funds

98

A training accident at Pau, France, where many of the members of the Lafayette Escadrille were taught to fly. Two Nieuports met in the middle of the field; on the left, one of the pilots sits, dazed, on a crumpled wing. To the far right, the other pilot has begun an explanation          U. S. AIR FORCE

for monthly allowances, uniforms, distribution of prizes, printing of pamphlets, etc."

The prizes included cash awards for having received decorations, running from 1,500 francs (about $300) for the Legion of Honor to 200 francs ($50) for additional citations (palms). Just why the French officials finally dropped their objections to the formation of such a unit has never been made clear. However, it was to become obvious that the propaganda value of Americans participating in the war was worth all the trouble to the French. In the phrase of Dr. Gros they were in "the vanguard of other great hosts that would come from America some day."

The unit came into being officially, on March 14, 1916 as Escadrille N. 124. Captain Georges Thénault was in command; second in command was Lt. Alfred de Laage de Meux. The seven original American members were Norman Prince, William Thaw, Elliot Cowdin (a Harvard graduate, from a wealthy family), Victor Chapman, Kiffin Rockwell, James McConnell (a Southern writer who originally served in Ambulance Corps) and Bert Hall. Of them all, possibly only the latter was motivated by a realistic outlook. A professional soldier, Hall could hardly have held illusions about the war's romantic aspects. A one-time con man (who worked in partnership with a girl companion and who may have spent some time in jail), Hall was reluctant to talk about his earlier background. In fact, he claimed several different Southern

99

The salvage hangar at Pau, 1916, where the trainers—Nieuports and Blériots—went after student mishaps          U. S. AIR FORCE

states as his home. He was hardly cut of the same gentlemanly cloth as were so many other members of the Lafayette Escadrille. A sharp cardplayer, an indifferent debtor, Hall apparently spoke the language of the soldier of fortune, for at least one of his squadron members recalled that he had a mouth like "a sewer." In time Bert Hall was asked to leave the Lafayette Escadrille, undoubtedly for "ungentlemanly" behavior, and transferred to N. 103, where he served with his usual rough style and received citations from the French. Tiring of the war, Hall requested a transfer to the United States. Once back in the U.S., he never bothered to report in, having, no doubt, tired of the Great War. He was one of only three original Lafayette Escadrille members who would survive the war.

As word was spread about the special American escadrille, other Americans arranged for transfers from the Foreign Legion and ambulance service also; others enlisted in the United States. In time, the original seven were joined by such men as Lawrence Rumsay, "a noted polo player of Buffalo," according to writer Laurence La Tourette Driggs; Clyde Balsley, Dudley Hill, Charles Chouteau Johnson (all from the ambulance corps); they were joined by Raoul Lufbery, Didier Masson (both of whom, though American citizens, were equally French, having lived away from their native land). Others to join were Paul Pevelka; Dennis Dowd, of Brooklyn, who, like so many hopeful fliers, died in a training crash before he reached the front; Robert Soubiran and many others. Before long the list became too lengthy for a mere

The original members of the Lafayette Escadrille: Kiffin Rockwell, Captain Georges
Thénault, Norman Prince, Lt. Alfred de Laage de Meux, Elliot Cowdin, Bert Hall
(in a black engineer's uniform), James McConnell and Victor Chapman. Not visible
is William Thaw (behind Thénault). The photo was taken at Luxeuil-les-Bains
when the Lafayette began operations          CULVER PICTURES

squadron; eventually, when the United States became a participant, the Lafayette Flying Corps, as it had by then become known, was absorbed into the
American Air Service.

It was, however, the original group which so early captured the imagination of the American people and undoubtedly helped those "back home" to
become accustomed to the idea of their boys fighting Over There.

The problem of financing was solved when the persuasive Dr. Gros called
upon Mr. and Mrs. W. K. Vanderbilt. "We spoke with warmth of our plans,"
Gros wrote shortly afterward. "Our enthusiasm must have been contagious,
for when I appealed for funds, Mrs. Vanderbilt walked to her desk and wrote
out a check for five thousand dollars—and turning to her husband said: 'Now,
K., what will you do?' His check read fifteen thousand dollars. With this sum
in hand, it looked as though our dream was really coming true!"

Following the customary period of training, generally at the great flying
school at Pau, the Americans were sent to their airdrome at Luxeuil. After
a few familiarity patrols led by Captain Thénault, the new unit was thought
to be ready for combat. Flying the latest Nieuports, the Lafayette Escadrille

101

Lieutenant de Laage seated in the Morane Bullet in which he was later killed in an accidental crash                                        U. S. AIR FORCE

very quickly found itself in the Battle of Verdun. Kiffin Rockwell scored the first victory, shooting down a German observation plane with four rounds of ammunition. After two weeks or so of flying near the critical Verdun sector, the Lafayette Escadrille was moved to the Bar-le-Duc Airdrome, closer to the battle zone, where it shared the facilities with Escadrille N. 3 (Guynemer, Dorme, Heurtaux) and Escadrille N. 65 (Nungesser). The young Americans were flying in fast company indeed.

They were flying *against* fast company also, for Oswald Boelcke had by this time been transferred to Verdun.

"This flying," Victor Chapman wrote enthusiastically to his father just twenty-two days before he was killed, "is much too romantic to be real modern war with all its horrors." Chapman fought with much the same audacity as did Guynemer and Nungesser and soon became a favorite of the French. He sought out combat with an almost reckless indifference. One of his many citations commented upon how he was "constantly hurling himself upon enemy aeroplanes without regard to their number or their altitude. On May 24th [1916] he attacked alone three German machines during which combat he had his clothing cut with many bullets and received a wound in the arm."

On June 16, Chapman received a head wound in a battle with Boelcke's unit. The following day, Clyde Balsley was led over the front for the first time; on the 18th of June, Balsley engaged in his first combat in company with Thénault, Prince and Rockwell. Balsley went down with a bullet through his stomach which exploded against his backbone. He crash-landed near some French trenches and though his Nieuport was demolished, Balsley survived.

102

Surgeons removed eleven fragments of the explosive bullet from his body. (Balsley lived, despite the seriousness of his wound, returned to the United States and never flew again.)

Because he was unable to eat normally, Balsley was visited regularly by Chapman, who came to deliver liquids (champagne and oranges, for their juice). On June 23, Chapman, his head still in bandages, set out from Bar-le-Duc on a regular patrol with Thénault, Prince and Lufbery; he had already flown his own patrols for the day. But he had a basket of oranges which he wanted to deliver to Clyde Balsley. Thénault practically ordered Chapman not to accompany the flight, but the American attached himself to the little formation after he took off.

Exactly what happened next is not known. Thénault sighted two German observation planes over the lines and led Prince and Lufbery in for the attack. They barely had time to fire a few rounds when several German planes swooped down from a cloud cover above the observation machines. Wisely appraising the situation—for they were both outnumbered and too far from their own lines—Thénault signaled for a withdrawal.

All the while, none had seen Chapman in his Nieuport. According to one witness, a French pilot, a single Nieuport fought with a group of German planes and then nosed down and crashed into the ground. Whether it was because he had been shot (as the Germans later reported) or because of structural failure of his plane has never been determined.

Victor Chapman was the first of the Lafayette to die for France. His death released an outpouring of emotion, both in France and the United States. Chapman's plane had crashed behind the German lines and he was given the usual hero's burial there. But funeral services in both France and America were held, significantly, on July 4. Thénault, writing to Chapman's family, said, "Our grief was extreme for we loved him deeply. At the moments of greatest danger in the air we could always discover the silhouette of his machine, that machine which he managed with so much ease. One of my *pilotes* has just said to me, 'Would that I had fallen instead of him.' "

A friend wrote: "I have just left the Church in the Avenue d'Alma, after attending the service in honor of your son. The ceremony was very touching in its simplicity. . . . The women about me were in tears. It was a sad celebration of your Independence Day, and brought home to me the beauty of heroic death and the meaning of life."

Messages arrived from Prime Minister Aristide Briand, who referred to Victor Chapman as "the living symbol of American idealism." The President of the French Republic, Raymond Poincaré sent a telegram of sympathy pointing out that Chapman had given his life "in the most just of all causes . . . ." The Boston *Transcript,* reflecting upon some of the emotion Chapman's death inspired in his still neutral native land, printed a letter from one of his former Harvard classmates, John Temple Jeffries, who found that Chapman's death was "the loss of a man who had all the noble and chivalrous instincts in such overwhelming proportions that it was literally impossible for him to act like the average person. It was as though Prince Rupert or Richard Plantagenet himself had stepped down from history. Chapman never could bridle his intrepidity enough to avoid all rows, and he never could suppress chivalry. . . ."

Kiffin Rockwell, Chapman's best friend, expressed his own, as well as his friend's point of view when writing to John J. Chapman:

> He died the most glorious death, and at the most glorious time of life [Chapman was twenty-seven] to die, especially for him with his ideals. I have never once regretted it for him, as I know he was willing and satisfied to give his life that way if it was necessary, and that he had no fear of death, and there is nothing to fear in death. . . . Yet he is not dead, he lives forever in every place he has been, and in everyone who knew him, and in the future generations little points of his character will be passed along. He is alive every day in this Escadrille and has a tremendous influence on all our actions.

Chapman's death, even more than the meticulously reported exploits of the Lafayette Escadrille, dramatized "the most just of all causes," and served to sway American sentiment toward the side of the Allies. It accelerated enlistments too, for more Americans were attempting to get into the celebrated Escadrille. The proximity of death was no deterrent. As Rockwell had written, Chapman had been lost "at the most glorious time of life to die." And what a way to die! The Nieuport, its wings collapsed, careening to earth. To the eager men trying to get into this famous organization, this seemed to be the only way to die in a just cause.

Over Verdun the men of the Lafayette fought with the desperate Germans. Late in August, Norman Prince distinguished himself by attacking a two-seater, an Aviatik, killing the observer and forcing the pilot to land the plane behind the French lines. Despite the intense activity, the Americans had been quite lucky; only Chapman had been killed and Balsley wounded.

By September, when the German push at Verdun had lost its momentum, Rockwell had gained four victories (Lufbery, who would be the "ace" of the Lafayette Escadrille, had twice as many). The unit was moved from the airdrome at Bar-le-Duc, given a week's leave in Paris and then ordered to report back at their original drome at Luxeuil. There was disappointment, for the men had hoped to join the British and French in the Somme offensive.

Re-outfitted with the latest model Nieuports, the men began preparing for a bombing mission into Germany to strike the Mauser munitions factories at Oberndorf.

They spent their time familiarizing themselves with their new machines and having their guns sighted. On September 23, Lufbery and Rockwell took off to try out their new planes, not knowing that the Germans, suspecting some sort of offensive action in the sector, consequently had large Fokker flights patrolling the area near Luxeuil.

The two Nieuports became separated in the clouds. Lufbery was a master of "cloud fighting," the use of clouds as a hiding place from which to jump an enemy plane. He found one, a two-seater, which he attacked—only to be attacked himself by a Fokker swarm for which the two-seater had been a decoy. Although his plane was badly shot up, Lufbery was able to extricate himself from the hopeless situation and landed on the first French field he could find.

Rockwell, too, had sighted a plane and dived into the attack; coolly he refrained from firing until he was within range. The German plane began firing first. Still on course, Rockwell flew directly toward the source of machine-gun fire; not until he was barely fifty yards away did he begin shooting. Men on the ground could see puffs of smoke emitting from the machine guns; Rockwell's Nieuport continued diving. The German plane was forced to swerve to avoid being hit. The Nieuport flashed by, still with nose pointed down; then a wing snapped off and fluttered end over end behind the plane. The plane plummeted into the ground an eighth of a mile behind the French lines.

Although the Nieuport, a delicate though formidable fighting plane, had a reputation for shedding wings in steep dives, Rockwell apparently had been hit in the chest by the German gunner and was dead when he hit the ground. His body was returned to Luxeuil wrapped in a French flag and his funeral was attended by Rockwell's squadron mates as well as by British and French flyers. "The best and bravest of us all is no more," Captain Thénault eulogized. "When Rockwell was in the air no German passed, and he was in the air most of the time."

As for his epitaph, Rockwell had written that himself when he wrote to his mother, "If I die I wish you to know that I died as all men should die—for that which is just."

Just as he had joined Rockwell in a grudge hunt for "Huns" after Victor Chapman had been killed, Lufbery teamed up with Norman Prince to avenge the death of Kiffin Rockwell.

It was on the bombing mission to Oberndorf (October 12, 1916), one of the first strategic raids in history, that Lufbery shot down his fifth plane and became an ace. The Lafayette Escadrille had been selected to fly as escort for the force of eighty French and British bombers. Among those from the unit were Lufbery, Prince, Didier Masson and de Laage. The mission had been carefully planned so that as much protection as possible was given the bombers over the hundred-and-fifty-mile trip. The escorting fighter planes were detailed to "clear the path of obstacles." Lufbery accounted for one of them, a Fokker, and became an ace. Prince also shot one down; he too was now an ace.

The two new aces flew a long day, landing when their fuel ran out. Gassing up, they took off again to protect the bombers on the homeward journey. Prince and Lufbery remained in the air even after the light had begun to fade. Not until they were certain that the last bomber had come home did

Dudley Hill, of the Lafayette Escadrille, standing beside his Nieuport. Armament of this plane consisted of a Lewis machine gun on the upper wing and a Vickers synchronized to fire through the propeller          U. S. AIR FORCE

they decide to land in a small emergency field at Corcieux (they did not have fuel enough to return to Luxeuil).

Lufbery landed first, and as he pulled his Nieuport out of the way Prince began his descent. In the dim light Prince did not see a line of electric wires

Sgt. Robert Soubiran at Cachy Airdrome in the Somme sector. An amateur photographer, Soubiran took practically all of the Lafayette Escadrille photos which appear in this book. Soubiran later commanded the 103 Aero Squadron, U. S. Air Service, when the Lafayette Escadrille was absorbed by the U. S. Army

that bordered one end of the strange field. His landing gear caught in the line, flipped over and as Lufbery watched in horror, Prince's plane whirled over, tossing him to the ground.

Lufbery ran to the crash and found Prince still conscious, although both his legs were broken and he suffered serious internal injuries. Before he fainted, Prince told those around him to light flares so that other planes attempting to land would see the wires. In the hospital, Prince was promoted to the rank of honorary lieutenant and given the Legion of Honor. He died three days later.

When the squadron moved into the Somme sector a few days afterward, they left their founder buried beside Kiffin Rockwell at Luxeuil. Norman Prince was the third of the original seven Lafayette Escadrille members to die. During this period the ranks of the Escadrille grew as more and more Americans, reading of the heroic exploits of Rockwell, Prince, Lufbery, Hall and the others, joined. Another Prince, Norman's brother Frederick, accompanied the unit to the Somme. During the latter months of 1916 some of the new members included Paul A. Rockwell (the brother of Kiffin), James Norman Hall (no relation to Bert Hall; later he wrote *The Lafayette Flying Corps* and the *Mutiny on the Bounty* trilogy with Charles Nordhoff), Kenneth Marr,

Nungesser, the great French ace, in Bar-le-Duc visiting members of the Lafayette Escadrille. On the extreme left is Norman ("Nimmy") Prince and on the extreme right, Didier Masson, who received a taste of aerial warfare during the Mexican Revolution (1913), when he served as the entire Mexican Air Force in a single plane     JARRETT COLLECTION

Harold B. Willis, Douglas MacMonagle, Edwin C. Parsons and dozens of others.

To newspaper readers in 1916 it must have seemed that the aerial war was being fought only by the Germans, the French and the Lafayette Escadrille. For the British continued to be curiously reticent about their airmen, and the High Command seemed to view their accomplishments with an objective eye commensurate with their strategic contribution. But for sheer intrepidity, the British pilots were unequaled. The French fought with élan, the Americans with headlong consecration, the Germans with crafty care and the British with guts.

It would have been difficult for the British to neglect the shooting down of the LZ-37 by the Royal Naval Air Service sublieutenant R. A. J. Warneford over Belgium either as an individual exploit or as a morale booster. The names of Boelcke, Immelmann, von Richthofen, Guynemer and Nungesser were better known to the British public in 1916 than W. B. Rhodes-Moorehouse, Lanoe G. Hawker, A. J. Liddell, G. S. M. Insall, R. B. Davis and L. W. B. Rees—all recipients of the Victoria Cross and all more or less anonymous British airmen.

And then along came Captain Albert Ball, who was destined to remove the basket which the British High Command had placed over the dazzling exploits of the British pilots. Exponent of the British school of fighting in its

Captain Albert Ball seated in the cockpit of his SE-5, one of the outstanding British "scout" aircraft. The Lewis machine gun may be seen mounted on the upper wing. It could be pulled down the quadrant mounting and rearmed in flight. It could also be fired at an angle—a favorite tactic of Ball's, who liked to come in underneath a German plane and spray it with bullets before the pilot was aware of the presence of a British plane          IMPERIAL WAR MUSEUM, LONDON

most individual expression, Albert Ball was the eldest son of a former Mayor of Nottingham.

A captain and flight leader by the time he was nineteen, Albert Ball looked more like a high school football hero than England's first air celebrity. As a boy he had displayed a fondness for guns and a flair for engineering. He was also interested in music and played the violin. The author Cecil Lewis, a one-time squadron mate of Ball's, commented upon this musical inclination and at the same time pointed out a curious disparity in Ball's makeup. "Ball was a quiet, simple little man," Lewis noted in his fine book *Sagittarius Rising*. "His one relaxation was the violin, and his favorite after-dinner amusement was to light a red magnesium flare outside his hut and walk around it in his pajamas, fiddling!"

Another of Ball's pastimes was gardening. After he had arrived in France, Ball wrote to his father asking to be sent some seeds, which he planted in an area he had fenced off near his living quarters. Ball kept his family posted on the progress of his garden more faithfully than he did on his flying.

Georges Guynemer, in a Spad, warming up at Cachy to take off during the Somme battle. The Lafayette Escadrille was also based at Cachy    U. S. AIR FORCE

The opening of the war found Ball floundering around in his own engineering firm; shortly afterward, he enlisted in a local regiment, the Sherwood Foresters. Finding the ground duties unexciting, Ball learned to fly at his own expense, and on October 15, 1915, earned his pilot's certificate—Number 1898—at the Ruffy-Beaumann School at Hendon.

Though headstrong and willing, Ball was not a natural flier (he had cracked up one plane while learning to fly). It was not until February 1916 that he was posted to No. 13 Squadron in France to pilot B. E. 2cs. The slow, artillery-spotting reconnaissance plane was not a favorite of Ball's, who once shocked no less a personage than R.F.C. Commander Trenchard, who had asked Ball what he thought of the B. E. "Bloody awful," was Ball's reply.

It was not until he was given a little Nieuport that Ball exhibited the same blunt determination in combat that he did in his speech. He had gained much-needed flying experience in the B. E.s as well as in a Bristol Scout and had displayed a willingness to partake in dangerous assignments such as flying spies behind the enemy lines. Obviously a pilot with Ball's aggressive temperament would be better flying a fighter plane. On May 7, 1916, he was transferred to No. 11 Squadron, commanded by Major W. H. Hubbard, and assigned a Nieuport. Ball's function would be to tag along on the two-seater missions to help protect the Quirks, which he had once flown and despised.

The Nieuport Scout of 1916 suited Ball perfectly. Though quite fragile and

110

small (the wingspan was 27 feet), the plane carried a Lewis machine gun mounted atop the upper wing which could fire forward and over the propeller arc. The gun was actuated by means of a cord which dangled into the cockpit. Some Nieuports also came equipped with mountings for Le Prieur rockets on the "vee" struts between the wings. These were fired electrically and, although sometimes used against aircraft, their prime function was for balloon attack.

Ball, himself small (he was short though powerfully built), fitted into the little French fighter plane perfectly. The man and machine complemented one another, each being equally unpredictable and suited to war. And each shared individual idiosyncracies with the blazing meteors.

"Of the great fighting pilots his tactics were the least cunning," wrote Cecil Lewis of Ball. "Absolutely fearless, the odds made no difference. He would always attack, single out his man, and close. On several occasions he almost rammed the enemy, and often came back with his machine shot to pieces." The French paid him the great compliment of calling him the "English Guynemer," for the fighting styles of the two men were similar. Both preferred working alone, although personal motivations were undoubtedly different: Guynemer seemed transfixed when he got into his machine, Ball was more simply full of fight.

His first official victory came on June 25, 1916, although he had probably accounted for one Albatros destroyed and an L.V.G. forced down the previous month. In company with five other Nieuports, Ball took off from Savy airdrome in the Somme sector to attack a line of *drachen,* the kite balloons which kept the Germans informed of the British activity on the ground. They were alerting their ground forces to the elaborate preparations for the British Somme offensive; almost two dozen of the fat little sausagelike balloons were strung out above the lines.

Some of the attacking Nieuports were fitted with Le Prieur rocket launchers, but Ball flew one which dropped little phosphorus bombs. Attacking *drachen* was not a popular sport, for their positions were ringed with guns, all precisely set for the correct range. Often, too, the German scouts flew in to defend the balloons. As soon as enemy fighter planes were sighted, the ground crews began winching in the balloon; if an attacking pilot dived in, surprising everyone, the occupant of the balloon would take to his parachute before he could be winched down. (Curiously, through most of the war only the balloonists used parachutes; fighter pilots seemed to regard them as unsportsmanlike or effeminate. This attitude accounted for many unnecessary deaths. The chutes were also too bulky to fit into the tiny cockpit. By 1918, however, some German pilots condescended to wear parachutes.)

When Ball and the other British pilots attacked their assigned cluster of balloons, the *drachen* were already bobbing and swaying as the ground crews wound them down. Four were hit by rockets and smudged the sky with the oily black smoke and orange flame as the balloons fluttered down around the dispersing men below. Ball picked out a likely victim, released his bombs—and missed. Chagrined and angry, he acted in characteristic fashion. Return-

Nieuports of the Lafayette Escadrille at Cachy, 1916

ing to Savy, he had his gun reloaded, asked for permission to return to the balloon line and took off again.

The *drachen* had been raised again, and the German gun crews were even more alert than usual. But Ball flew through machine-gun fire and the "flaming onions" (incendiary bullets which could be seen, and frequently dodged); his Nieuport was hit and bits of fabric blew into the slipstream. An ominous sound came from the engine, which had taken a hit. It is unlikely that the determined Ball was conscious of anything but the gasbag in his sights; when it loomed large he pulled the trigger cable and swooped by. Looking back he was elated to see the glow of small flame and then the sudden eruption and collapse of the balloon. Ball then hurried back to his home base. He had scored his first "official," his first—and last—balloon.

Ball was not a scientific fighter in the manner of such methodical tacticians as René Fonck, Richthofen, Edward Mannock and Rickenbacker; Ball was a plunger. He thought nothing of throwing his little Nieuport directly into the path of a German formation of seven or even more aircraft. It is possible, despite his youth (Ball was not yet twenty when his fighting career opened), that he was aware of the confusion such an action would cause, and of the advantage it would bring to the more aggressive pilot. A more devious approach, also practiced by Ball, was to bring his Nieuport underneath the enemy aircraft (generally after scattering the formation with one of his frontal attacks), just below and behind the tail. This was a blind spot, even in two-seaters. From this position Ball would spray the underside of the German plane from dangerously close quarters (sometimes from as little as fifteen

112

yards away). The result was, at best, that the German plane went down, often with the pilot never knowing what hit him; at the worst, Ball's technique meant that he would return from a patrol with a badly shot-up aircraft.

His performances won him many citations, although he himself did not seem impressed with his mounting list of victories. Nor was he exhilarated by it all and he frequently complained, in his letters to his family, of "feeling wonky." His father, in typical civilian (noncombatants are frequently more bloodthirsty than soldiers) fashion, tried to cheer the boy up, urging him to "Let the devils have it."

"Yes," his son replied, "I always let them have it all I can, but really I don't think them devils. I only scrap because it is my duty, but I do not think anything about the Hun. He is just a good chap with very little guts, trying to do his best. Nothing makes me feel more rotten than to see them go down."

But down they went, nonetheless. By the time he was withdrawn from combat for duty in England, Ball had destroyed ten enemy aircraft, using harrowing tactics that may very well have frightened some Germans to death. He had forced another twenty planes down more or less intact. One of his citations (dated 16 September 1916) emphasized Ball's "Remarkable bravery and skill."

> Observing a group of seven enemy aeroplanes in battle formation, he attacked one instantly at less than fifteen yards and brought it down. The others took flight. Continuing his patrol he saw five machines; he approached one of them until he was less than ten yards distant and brought it down. He attacked another of them, riddled it with bullets and brought it down. Then he went back to the nearest aerodrome for more ammunition. He set out again, attacked three new enemy aeroplanes and brought them down out of control. Having no more fuel he returned with his machine riddled with bullets.

Ball's own reports of his engagements were much less given over to color. Nor was he apt to exaggerate. The entire narrative of a report he filed on July 3, 1916, when he was sent out on a special mission to get a German observation balloon, read:

> Nieuport Scout A. 134 crossed the lines at 5,000 ft. and went towards Balloon. When within ¼ mile Balloon was being hauled down. Nieuport fired darts when within 16 yards and immediately afterwards emptied drum of Buckingham [incendiary] Bullets at Balloon. Darts missed, Buckinghams mostly hit but did not ignite Balloon, which was hauled down to ground apparently uninjured.

Such reticence and daring won Ball the admiration of his fellow pilots, although his reputation as a lone wolf would have hardly made him a popular member of a team—as the fighting squadrons were beginning to evolve into around this time. One of his admirers was William A. Bishop, a Canadian,

113

Walter Lovett, Edmond C. Genêt, Raoul Lufbery and James McConnell, all of the Lafayette Escadrille, studying a device which contains a map on rollers for use in aircraft U. S. AIR FORCE

who was one of the last of the individualists. He related one of Ball's most remarkable adventures.

Ball had gone off on one of his lone patrols and was twenty miles inside the German lines where he encountered two German planes. "Without hesitation he flew straight at these two and engaged them in a flight which lasted over ten minutes," Bishop later recalled. Having used up his ammunition, Ball began firing at the two German planes with his pistol. The German pilots had had enough of such sky fighting and dived away from the Englishman. Disgusted, Ball "seized a piece of paper and pencil which he had with him," Bishop continued, "and wrote out a challenge for the same two machines to meet him at the same spot the next day.

"At the appointed time Ball turned up on the spot and a few minutes later the same two enemy machines approached him from the east. He flew toward them to engage in a fight, but at that moment three more of the enemy came down from the sky and attacked him. It was a carefully laid trap and he had fallen into it. . . .

"The three machines that had attacked him from behind were of the latest fighting type and were all flown by expert men. At every turn Ball, who was

114

William Mitchell (third from right) visits the Lafayette Escadrille. To Mitchell's right are Captain Thénault and William Thaw. Mitchell was on an inspection tour, studying the latest aerial combat techniques          U. S. AIR FORCE

underneath and was thus at a slight disadvantage, found himself outmaneuvered. Turn and twist as he would, he always found one of the enemy on top of him and another just ready to catch him if he turned the other way. Several times bullets passed within inches of him."

Hemmed in almost hopelessly and well away from his own lines, Ball realized he would have to think of something; he could not fight his way out. He dived for the ground and landed in a large field.

The three German planes followed him down. They had recognized the plane and, of course, bringing down so celebrated a pilot as Albert Ball would merit much official attention. The remaining two planes raced for their own airdrome to spread the good word.

Having landed, the three eager German pilots left their planes and raced for Ball's Nieuport. Obviously the pilot was injured, for the plane had come to a halt and the propeller was still whirling, although slowly. When the Germans were well away from their own planes, and the other two planes had left the skies above, Ball—who had not been hit at all—took off, leaving behind three very embarrassed and no longer victorious pilots.

So effective a fighter pilot was extremely valuable and Ball was properly rewarded with the Military Cross and the Distinguished Service Order, among

Capt. Lanoe G. Hawker, one of Britain's first and finest airmen. He was killed in an aerial duel with von Richthofen     IMPERIAL WAR MUSEUM, LONDON

other decorations, and brought home to lecture to embryo pilots in British flying schools. Around this time another British pilot, James Thomas Byford McCudden, began making a name for himself, and Edward Mannock transferred from the Royal Engineers into the R.F.C. Though he had astigmatism of the left eye, Mannock managed to pass the eye examination. This intense, afflicted man would end as the British ace of aces with 73 victories.

The preoccupation with the sporting aspect of air fighting, with the accumulation of heads and trophies, tended to obscure the work of the more sedate, less spectacular airmen. The man Richthofen called "the English Boelcke," and whom he killed, Lanoe George Hawker, was more typical of the airman concerned with finishing the war than with his own personal victory list. He was also an outstanding pilot with rare qualities of leadership and technical ability. He was credited with initiating several mechanical innovations, such as the ring gunsight, and also conceived the idea of issuing pilots fur-lined flight boots as protection from the severe cold at the altitude at which they often flew. No one had thought of that problem in the war's early phase.

A prewar pilot of great skill, Hawker was among the first British pilots to fly over the Western Front. He served first with No. 6 Squadron, R.F.C.,

116

flying R.E. 5s and B. E. 2cs. In the latter, the infamous Quirks of the Fokker Fodder period, Hawker set out on April 18, 1915, to bomb the German Zeppelin shed at Gontrode. Before attending to the shed, Hawker, while under fire from a ground gunner, attacked a balloon with small bombs and hand grenades. After finally puncturing the kite balloon with a grenade, Hawker dropped his last bomb on the shed, which went up in flames. Hawker returned to his base in France with over thirty gunshot holes in his Quirk.

By the summer, Hawker was flying the Bristol Scout, which had a single-shot cavalry rifle mounted on the fuselage and which angled outward to miss the propeller. He then set up a system along the front whereby as soon as a German plane appeared over the front the word would be telephoned to No. 6 Squadron and Hawker would immediately take off to challenge the intruder. During the early phases of the war Hawker shot down many enemy aircraft, although this occurred before it became the fashion to keep score (Hawker's final total, officially, was nine, but he undoubtedly accounted for more than triple that number).

If he was not exciting anyone back home, Hawker was certainly impressing "Tommy" in the trenches with his tactics, and his little Bristol Scout was a popular aircraft. Its appearence meant that Tommy would be less harassed by accurately directed artillery fire and trench strafing.

For his deep raid into enemy territory to burn the Zeppelin shed at Gontrode, Hawker did, however, receive official recognition in the form of the Distinguished Service Order.

He was awarded the Victoria Cross for his performance of July 1, 1915. His infantry outposts alerted Hawker of the presence of an Aviatik over the lines. Leaping into his Bristol, the Englishman took off in the company of Lt. L. A. Strange (who was as aggressive a fighter as Hawker and will be recalled as the pilot who had been tossed out of his plane over the front and left hanging onto his gun). Strange, in his slower Martinsyde, was to serve as a decoy while Hawker attended to the German plane. The ruse worked, for Hawker pounced upon the Aviatik as it attempted to knock down Strange and sent it down burning behind its own lines. Later in the day Hawker took off alone and attacked a Rumpler which suffered engine damage and crashed within Allied lines. Satisfied that he had taken care of that intruder, Hawker climbed to 11,000 feet into the glare of the sun. An unsuspecting Albatros two-seater came within view shortly after and Hawker dropped down upon the hapless Germans and sent down his third plane of the day. The gun he carried was a single-shot weapon so that Hawker was obliged to reload it after every firing; that he could hit anything with the crude manner in which it was mounted beside the cockpit was a miracle (later Bristol Scouts had a Lewis machine gun atop the upper wing). A triple victory in a single day was unusual in the early months of the war and Hawker was given the V.C. for this remarkable feat.

He was also brought back to England to form and lead Number 24 Squadron, which was to be equipped with the new De Haviland 2s, Britain's answer

The *drachen*, a German observation balloon. Balloons were employed by both sides for observation and directing field artillery fire. Ground troops hated them and airmen found them suicidal targets because of the heavy ring of antiaircraft guns which protected them. "Balloon busters" were highly respected by other airmen though a bit mad                                                            JARRETT COLLECTION

to the Fokker. The D.H. had the advantage of an unobstructed view for the forward-firing Lewis gun. The plane was a pusher type with the propeller mounted behind the fuselage; while it handled well, it was not an outstanding fighter plane, being neither particularly fast (about 90 mph at best) nor maneuverable. Even so, the D.H. 2 was superior to the Fokker Eindekkers and proved itself during the Battle of the Somme.

No. 24 Squadron, with Hawker in command, moved to France and was set up at Bertangles to begin its operations. It was the first British single-seater squadron in France. Their job was to serve as patrol and escort planes along the Western Front, engaging the German planes in combat whenever possible and to bring an end to the legend of the invincibility of the Fokker. It was in a skirmish with members of No. 24 Squadron that Boelcke was killed.

Hawker's last flight took place on November 23, 1916. He was by then Britain's most famous airman—at least along the front. Still flying the now

A Bristol Bullet, Model D scouting plane. One of the finest British aircraft of the war, the plane's usefulness as a fighter was handicapped because it was not equipped with a forward-firing gun.                                              U. S. AIR FORCE

outmoded D.H. 2s (which were afflicted with engine troubles), Hawker had taken off as a member of a flight of four D.H. 2s led by Capt. J. O. Andrews. Hawker, a major and the squadron commander, had come along as an ordinary member of the flight.

They ran into a formation of five Albatros scouts of the Boelcke Staffel. The German planes, which were slightly below the British planes, turned toward their own lines in order to gain altitude, then turned again to give battle.

The British patrol had already been decimated by the engine troubles of two of their planes, forcing the pilots to return to their base. Hawker and Andrews, however, continued in pursuit of the German planes. Each singled out a machine and began firing. Hawker had picked an all-red Albatros for an adversary and soon was on the German's tail and fired a burst.

Andrews, too, had taken position behind one of the German planes and had begun firing when he himself was attacked from behind by another Albatros. A stream of bullets struck the D.H. in the engine, which immediately began misfiring, and Andrews was forced to leave the fight. He dropped toward the British lines and managed to bring his smoking plane down near Gillemony.

Hawker was now alone, over the German lines. His adversary was a good pilot, almost as good as Hawker, and the two planes—apparently uninterrupted by the other German fighters—dueled in the sky above the trenches, twisting and turning, each trying to get on the tail of the other.

119

The nose of a D.H. 2 of No. 2 Squadron, R.F.C., commanded by Lanoe G. Hawker. Struck by an antiaircraft shell, the plane was brought back by its pilot, D. M. Tidmarsh                                        U. S. AIR FORCE

One of the natural hazards with which the Allied airmen had to contend was the prevailing winds which blew from the Allied lines toward the German-held territory. Any extended dogfight invariably drifted over the German lines; one of the reasons that, even if hit, the German pilots were generally able to land in their own territory and escape capture. Also, it was easier for them to receive confirmation of their victories.

Neither pilot seemed able to get the final advantage over the other as the fight progressed. The Albatros was faster and could outclimb the D.H., but the English plane could turn faster; thus no decision was reached. On one close brush, Hawker waved at the German pilot. The battle drifted farther west from 10,000 feet down to nearly 3,000. Now low on fuel, Hawker realized that unless he left the combat he would never get back home. Wisely, he broke off and pointed the plane for France, ruddering from side to side to present a difficult-to-hit target. He was now only a few hundred feet above the ground. The red Albatros swooped in for the kill. "The battle is now close

120

The Sopwith 1½ Strutter (so-called because it had only a single set of interplane struts on each outer wing bay and the half-strut extending from the fuselage at the wing's center section). This plane was the first R.F.C. aircraft to be fitted with an efficient synchronization gear enabling the pilot to fire through the propeller in the direction of flight. The observer-gunner, in the rear seat, fired a Lewis gun mounted on a Scarff ring. The 1½ Strutter may also be the first plane equipped with flaps; the trailing edge of the lower wings carried so-called "air-brakes," similar to modern wing flaps. This plane was used by both the British and French

U. S. SIGNAL CORPS: NATIONAL ARCHIVES

to the ground," the German pilot later reported. "He [Hawker] is not a hundred yards above the earth. Our speed is terrific. He starts back for his front. He knows I am right behind him and close on his tail. He knows my gun barrel is trained on him. He starts to zigzag, making sudden darts right and left—right and left—confusing my aim and making it difficult to train my gun on him. But the moment is coming. I am fifty yards behind him. My machine gun is firing incessantly. We are hardly fifty yards above the ground— just skimming it.

"Now I am within thirty yards of him. He must fall. The gun pours out its stream of lead. Then it jams. Then it reopens fire. That jam almost saved his life. One bullet goes home. He is struck through the back of the head. His plane leaps and crashes down. It strikes the ground just as I swoop over. His machine gun rammed itself into the earth, and now it decorates the entrance over my door. He was a brave man, a sportsman and fighter."

Thus did the Baron von Richthofen report his eleventh victory, certain that, in some manner, he had avenged the death of Boelcke. He himself had not yet achieved anything near the celebrity that his teacher had; in fact, possibly only Mathy, of the Naval Airship Division, enjoyed the kind of adulation that had been given Boelcke.

Undaunted by the severe losses of 1915—ten airships—Strasser, commander of the German naval airships, continued to believe his arm would be able to bring England to its knees. "The performance of the big airships has reinforced my conviction that England can be overcome by means of airships," he stated in a secret memo to his chief, Vice Admiral Reinhard Scheer, "inasmuch as the country will be deprived of the means of existence through increasingly extensive destruction of cities, factory complexes, dockyards, harbor works with war and merchant ships lying therein, railroads, etc."

In essence, and on paper, Strasser's idea was a reasonably sound definition of strategic bombardment which was to have its most devastating exemplification in the Second World War. Crippling the enemy's war potential would, of necessity, shorten the war. Strasser's devotion to his airships, however, afflicted him with military myopia: the terror weapon was not so terrible. It was vulnerable, ungainly and easily fell victim to wind and weather. Snow and rain would add weight, forcing the airship to attack from perilously low altitudes, thus canceling out its major advantage over the outmoded aircraft generally assigned to defend the homeland and the antiaircraft guns. This was, of course, the advantage of height. Although Strasser sincerely believed that "the airships offer a certain means of victoriously ending the war," the climax of the airship campaign, which came in the winter of 1916, should have convinced him otherwise.

Of course, he would not have known that the damage claims made by his airship commanders were imprecise and exaggerated. Blown about in the upper reaches of sky, they often had no real idea where they dropped their bombs. Although generally extremely careful about attacking non-military targets, the Zeppelin commanders inadvertently did just that simply because they were fifty miles off course and bombed the wrong target. In the confusion, fear and at times almost unbearable cold, bombs were dropped into the sea, open fields or heavily populated areas—all in error. The cold, calculating Hun (or Uhlan) "baby killers" were as fictional as some of their own damage claims.

The 1916 campaign opened on January 31 with a characteristic flourish when nine ships took off to attack England, with the desirable target being the city of Liverpool on the west coast. Mathy, in his L-13, dropped some of his bombs on what he believed to be "blast furnaces and other extensive installations," but missed the city he thought he was hitting by fifteen miles. Ground fog and clouds were to interfere with the navigation and bombing of

The popular Sopwith Pup. This fighter was produced after the 1½ Strutter and was one of the favorite planes of the war. It was one of the few planes which could match performance with the Albatros, particularly because it was extremely maneuverable up to an altitude of 15,000 feet          U. S. AIR FORCE

all other Zeppelins on the raid. One of the airships, the L-19 under command of Odo Loewe, became lost and after wandering about over England, came down in the North Sea. The English trawler *King Stephen* came upon the airship, still afloat the next morning, and fearing that the L-19's crew could overpower his little crew of nine, the trawler's captain left the sixteen Germans to drown in the icy sea. Some months later a bottle was washed ashore on the Norwegian coast containing Loewe's final messages, one of which read: *My greetings to my wife and child. An English trawler was here and refused to take us aboard. She was the* King Stephen *and hailed from Grimsby.* The trawler was eventually sunk by the Germans, although captain and crew were spared.

The toll of airships varied directly with the intensity of their attempts to bring the war to England. On February 16, 1916, the defense of England from air attack reverted from the Admiralty to the War Office, the change resulting in the stiffening of antiaircraft defense; also, improved aircraft squadrons were established. The defense of the London area was assigned to No. 39 Squadron. Although the planes with which the defenders of London were expected to do battle with the great airships were hardly first-rate, the pilots were as aggressive as ever.

123

Antiaircraft gun emplacement; man at right is operating a range-finder

On March 31, seven airships made a try at attacking London. The German Zeppelins suffered the usual mechanical troubles and had other problems. The worst was the loss of the L-15, which had been under heavy antiaircraft fire over London. In addition, it was attacked from above by Lt. A. de Brandon in a rickety B.E. 2c, from which he dropped explosive darts. Badly punctured, the L-15 turned for home, but fell into the sea, limp and no longer majestic. The skipper, Joachim Breithaupt, and sixteen of his crew were taken prisoner; one man was lost when the L-15 sagged into the water, driving the gondola up into the framework. At first fired upon by one of the British trawlers which converged upon the L-15, the airship was further damaged by officers of the destroyer *Vulture;* it sank while being towed to port.

A sequel to this occurred on May 2, when eight airships set out hoping to hit the English fleet in the north of England. At least three of the ships

Lt. Leefe Robinson, who brought down a German Zeppelin before the eyes of Londoners on the night of September 3, 1916    IMPERIAL WAR MUSEUM, LONDON

wasted their bombs on an empty moor which burned a good deal of heather, and the L-20, after icing up in freezing squalls, became lost and finally came down in a Norwegian fjord. The airship campaign was clearly expensive. And with little resultant damage done to the enemy.

There were fatalities and destruction of property, although of minor military consequence. Londoners, instead of running amok in fear, stood around to watch the evening show—and no small number of injuries incurred during the Zeppelin raids could be attributed to falling shell fragments from English guns. If Strasser had overestimated the potential of his airships, he more than underestimated the tough Londoner. (A generation later, his successors would do the same.)

The spectators were finally treated to a good show on the night of September 2-3. The Germans hoped on that attack to stage an impressive Army-Navy operation. Strasser dispatched every operational airship at his command, twelve in all; the Army, which did not share Strasser's enthusiasm for the big ships, provided four: the LZ-90, LZ-97, LZ-98 and SL-11. The latter not a Zeppelin product, was manufactured by Schutte-Lanz of Mannheim-Rheinau, Zeppelin's chief rival. Its structure was mainly of laminated plywood. Strasser did not believe these ships to be "really combat-worthy," although the building of these ships was encouraged by the War Ministry as a competitor of Zeppelin.

On what was to be the greatest airship raid of the war, the craft encoun-

125

Wreckage of a German Army Zeppelin, the LZ-77, after being hit by an incendiary antiaircraft shell over Revigny in the Verdun sector. The German Army Airship Service preferred to use its aircraft in cooperation with the ground troops—as this airship was at the opening of the Verdun campaign—unlike the German naval air service, which advocated strategic bombardment of behind-the-lines cities and military installations          U. S. AIR FORCE

tered winds in their operational altitudes as well as rain and snow. Two ships did not bomb England at all and the remainder of the armada did not make an impressive showing (there were four deaths as a result of the raid, a dozen people were injured and damages exceeded £21,000).

Second Lt. William Leefe Robinson of No. 39 Squadron piloting an old B.E. 2, had taken off to intercept the Zeppelin raiders. He had seen one airship, the Army LZ-98, commanded by Ernst Lehmann, under heavy antiaircraft fire from the guns of Dartford and Tilbury (Lehmann actually thought he was over the London dock area), but it had dropped its bombs and slipped into the clouds, climbing, and escaped Leefe Robinson's attempt to attack.

Another army airship, the SL-11, was approaching London from the northwest and passed over St. Albans and by 1:20 A.M. the commander, Wilhelm Schramm, ordered the first bombs to be dropped. Searchlights and ground guns went into action and six planes from No. 39 Squadron wheezed and labored to reach the airship.

Leefe Robinson, having lost one opportunity, approached the SL-11 carefully. He noticed that the ground fire was quite inaccurate, bursting above,

126

The L-20, lost and out of fuel after an attempted raid on England on May 2, 1916, fell into the sea near Stavanger off the coast of Norway     U. S. AIR FORCE

below and behind the ship. Hoping the antiaircraft fire would be as kind to him, he made his first approach from about 800 feet below, firing a full drum of the new incendiary bullets along the length of the ship.

"It seemed to have no effect," he reported later. "I therefore moved to one side and gave it another drum distributed along its side—without apparent effect. I then got behind it (by this time I was very close—500 feet or less below) and concentrated one drum on one part (underneath rear). I was then at a height of 11,500 feet when attacking the Zeppelin. I had hardly finished the drum before I saw the part I fired at glow. When the third drum was fired there were no searchlights on the Zeppelin and no antiaircraft was firing. I quickly got out of the way of the falling blazing Zeppelin and being very excited, fired a few red Very lights and dropped a parachute flare."

To the other men in those airships within sight of the falling SL-11 it was an appalling and chilling conflagration. Sixteen men perished in the fire of the costly airship (about four times more than the amount of damage the entire raid had caused). It also marked the last attempt by the German army airships to attack England; within a year the service came to an end.

Strasser, however, continued to believe in his airships. The loss of the wooden, and in his opinion, inferior SL-11 proved nothing to him. With the coming on the next new moon phase when the skies would be dark, Strasser planned another large attack, using a dozen airships including four new so-called "super-Zeppelins" under the command of Mathy, the Zeppelin ace, in the L-31. Two other veterans were in command of two of the super-Zeppelins, Werner Peterson in the L-32 and Alois Böcker in the L-33. Neither was to return to his base that night.

Lt. A. de B. Brandon attacked the L-33; he was having trouble with his Lewis machine gun, which fell out of its mounting. Replacing the gun, Brandon turned again to attack the big airship, which had been struck by ground fire and was already in serious trouble. Although he did not set the L-33 afire, Brandon's attack undoubtedly helped bring it down. It crashed to earth in a field and after setting it afire, Böcker attempted to escape, but he and the other twenty-one crew members were captured. They were the fortunate ones of that evening's raid.

Around midnight Peterson, in the L-32, began his run on London at about 13,000 feet. Clamped in the glare of the searchlights and under heavy fire from the guns below, Peterson salvoed his bombs and turned east.

From below, a B.E. 2c flown by Lt. Frederick Sowrey "maneuvered into position. . . . The airship was well lighted by searchlights but there was not a sign of any gunfire. I could distinctly see the propellers revolving and the airship was maneuvering to avoid the searchlight beams. I fired at it."

Sowrey emptied two drums of ammunition into the airship and had begun on a third before he could see the incipient flickers here and there. Then it burst into flame and plunged to the ground and burned for three quarters of

All that remained of the German Zeppelin L-33 after it fell to earth at Colchester and was set afire by its commander, Alois Böcker, following a raid on London. The entire crew was imprisoned U. S. AIR FORCE

Prime Minister Lloyd-George (face partially obscured by framework), Foreign Secretary Arthur James Balfour and other British officials inspect the burned-out L-32 after it had been shot down by Lt. Frederick Sowrey. All on board were killed

U. S. AIR FORCE

an hour; all twenty-two men aboard died. According to one witness, one incinerated figure staggered out of the mass of wreckage screamed, *"Dreizehn!"* ("Thirteen"); it was Peterson, who had been on his thirteenth raid.

The effect of the disasters upon the morale of airship crews was evident— there seemed a morbid belief that it was only a matter of time before all would go in the same manner as Peterson and his crew. Only the courageous and skillful Mathy, whom they all admired and respected, seemed to bolster them. On the fateful raid of September 23-24, he in the L-31 had passed directly over London (the London toll was 37 dead, 114 injured). In his early thirties, the handsome Mathy was the hero of the airship service and regarded as the greatest of all commanders in the service. Despite the obvious failure of the Zeppelins, which now proved to be vulnerable even to the slow-flying Quirks, the determined Strasser pressed ahead with his plan to end the war with his airships.

Mathy led a formation of eleven Zeppelins on October 1, 1916. Winds and weather quickly canceled out three of the airships. Several others wandered over unrecognized sections of England looking for a place to drop their bombs. Ice impaired the performance of the ships and even the radio communications by coating the antennas. The L-21, iced up, flew at a tilt 10 de-

Kapitan Heinrich Mathy, greatest of the German airship commanders, who died in the flaming wreckage of the L-31 which crashed at Potters Bar, Middlesex

IMPERIAL WAR MUSEUM, LONDON

Capt. W. J. Tempest                    IMPERIAL WAR MUSEUM, LONDON

grees off the horizontal because of the weight of the ice. Robert Koch, in the L-24, was meandering through the clouds, but was able to fix on a star and then turned toward London. Above the city he saw an airship burning for a moment and then it crashed through the clouds and to the ground.

Earlier, Lt. W. J. Tempest had coaxed his B.E. 2c—a Quirk—off the ground at North Weald Basset and directed the plane toward London. He could see a Zeppelin at the apex of a pyramid of searchlights. He judged that it was about fifteen miles away and headed for London.

Tempest reported later:

> At first I drew near my objective very rapidly (as I was on one side of London and it was on the other, and both were heading for the center of the city): all the time I was having an extremely unpleasant time, as to get to the Zepp I had to pass through a very inferno of shells from the A. A. guns below.
>
> All at once it appeared to me that the Zeppelin must have sighted me, for she dropped all her bombs in one volley, swung around, tilted up her nose and proceeded to race away northward, climbing rapidly as

130

she went. At the time of the dropping of the bombs I judged her to be at an altitude of 11,500 feet. I made after her at full speed at about 15,000 feet altitude, gradually overhauling her. At this period the A. A. fire was intense, and I, being about five miles behind the Zeppelin, had an extremely uncomfortable time. At this point misfortune overtook me, for my mechanical pressure pump went wrong and I had to use my hand pump to keep up the pressure in my fuel tank. This exercise at so high an altitude was very exhausting, besides occupying an arm, thus giving me one hand less to operate with when I commenced to fire.

As I drew up with the Zeppelin, to my relief I found that I was free from A. A. fire, for the nearest shells were bursting quite three miles away. The Zeppelin was now nearly 15,000 feet high and mounting rapidly. I therefore decided to dive at her, for though I held a slight advantage in speed, she was climbing like a rocket and leaving me standing. I accordingly gave a tremendous pump to my fuel tank, and dived straight at her, firing as I came. I let her have another burst as I passed under her tail, and flying along underneath her, pumped lead into her for all I was worth. I could see tracer bullets flying from her in all directions, but I was too close under her for her to concentrate on me.

As I was firing, I noticed her begin to glow red inside like an enormous Chinese lantern, and then a flame shot out of the front part of her and I realized she was on fire. She then shot up about 200 feet, paused, and came roaring down straight on me before I had time to get out of the way. I nose-dived for all I was worth, with the Zepp tearing after me, and expected every minute to be engulfed in the flames. I put my machine into a spin and just managed to corkscrew out of the way as she shot past me roaring like a furnace. I righted my machine and watched her hit the ground with a shower of sparks.

I then proceeded to fire off dozens of green Very lights in my exuberance of my feelings.

His night's adventures, however, were not yet finished, for when he attempted to land on his fog-enshrouded field, Tempest crashed and cut his head on a machine gun.

The German airship fell into a field near Potters Bar, a flaming mass of twisted metal. Some distance away from it a man lay dying; he had apparently chosen to leap from the ship to escape the tortures of burning to death. The impact of his fall drove his body halfway into the ground. When his identification disc was examined by R.F.C. inspectors, it was found to read:

KAPTLT. MATHY
L 31

The greatest airship commander of the war was dead and, as one member of the service commented at the time, "with him the life and soul of our airship service went out too."

The year ended with further destruction to the Zeppelins both over London and even accidentally in their own sheds. In all, sixteen naval airships were lost during 1916 (six of them over England); but Strasser persisted in defending his fleet. Other minds seemed to favor leaving air fighting to aircraft, the great Gotha bombers were in readiness, and improved fighters were being sent to the *staffeln* along the Western Front. The time of the aces had come.

Warneford's Morane Parasol, with which he destroyed a German airship

# 1917

*I am not out for breaking records. Besides, generally speaking, we of the flying service do not think of records at all.*

—MANFRED VON RICHTHOFEN

The Albatros D-III, introduced to the front in January 1917. The first unit to fly this plane was Richthofen's Jagdstaffel 11. Because it was a better fighting aircraft than the Nieuports, Spad 7 and the Sopwith Pup, the Albatros D-III, flown by Germany's best pilots, was responsible for the period that came to be known as "Bloody April"

# The aces flourished

during 1917, those, that is, who survived long enough to fly the improved aircraft that came during that crucial year. The first aces, many of them neither very skilled pilots nor marksmen of any note, had managed to build up their scores and reputations almost purely on the strength of aggressive nerve. Few lived long enough to learn to fly; most, in fact, in the excellent phrase of Alexander McKee, "did not so much land, as arrive."

The aircraft of 1917 required skilled handling and were a marked advancement over the original warplanes of just three years before. The frail boxy stick-and-wire machines were superseded by planes of greater potency and toughness. Not all were equally excellent, and there was a constant behind-the-lines war in progress to surpass the enemy's aircraft. Superior planes meant a clear sky over the lines, free of trench-strafing, bombing and reconnaissance.

Germany held the advantage in late 1916 and through the spring of 1917, chiefly because the Albatros D-III was a better plane than the ones the British were using, obsolete B.E. 2s which were staunchly defended by the Royal Aircraft Factory. These planes, issued to the squadrons on the Western Front (although replacements for them already existed), were no match for the Albatros and Halberstadt Scouts and ushered in that dread period which British pilots named "Bloody April."

It should be emphasized that to the men flying the planes, they were not "crates," but, according to George A. Vaughn who served with both the British and American forces, "the very best we had at the time." Actually, pilots called their aircraft their "mounts," a throwback to cavalry tradition, or their "bus," or "taxi" (which is what Guynemer called his Nieuports and Spads). That they were anything but the most modern weapons of war was generally reflected in the attitudes of the airmen. The term "flaming coffin" was not employed by the British in referring to the DeHaviland 4, which when originally used in March 1917 proved itself to be a superior aircraft. (The pejorative name was coined by American units in 1918.)

Not that the men did not regard some of their planes as inferior. The British Royal Aircraft Factory, in stubbornly and blindly producing certain planes beyond their period of usefulness, placed the British pilots at a serious disadvantage. There were other disadvantages also. One, already mentioned, was the problem of the prevailing winds over the Western Front, which tended to drift the fighting planes over German-held territory. Another was that the Germans fought a defensive war which forced the British and the French to take the offensive. If a plane was not properly designed for the offense, the Albatroses and Halberstadts of the Germans simply cut them to ribbons.

The synchronized machine gun, developed in England by a Romanian inventor, George Constantinesco, was not introduced in any great numbers

135

unserer erfolgreichsten
Kampfflieger.

Vizefeldwebel Festner    Leutnant Schäfer

Leutnant Frhr. von Richthofen

Rittmeister Frhr. von Richthofen          Leutnant Wolff

511
Postkartenvertrieb V
BERLIN N.
Nachdruck wird gericht

German picture postcard. Gathered around their commander, Manfred von Richthofen (center) are Sebastian Festner, Emil Schaefer, the "Red Baron's" younger brother Lothar and Kurt Wolff          JARRETT COLLECTION

until the advent of the British S.E. 5, the Bristol Fighter and the Sopwith Camel, all of which did not appear on the front until after "Bloody April."

Organization was another factor, and by 1917 the German Air Service had formed its many Jagdstaffeln into integrated units with specific functions. These were the fighter units, which naturally received the most attention; there were also similarly organized ground attack units and bombardment squadrons. By April 1917 the originally projected thirty-seven fighter units were operational, most of them flying the Albatros D-III.

Many of the Jastas were, by early 1917, commanded by former members of Jasta Boelcke, with Jasta 11 under the command of Richthofen. He had received, on January 16, 1917, the *Ordre Pour le Mérite,* Germany's highest award, and shortly after reported at Douai on the Western Front to take over command of his own Jasta. Among the original members were Karl Allmenroder, Kurt Wolff, and later, Karl Emil Schaefer—all to become outstanding

136

airmen. Richthofen, of the aristocracy, was not as warm and likeable as had been his teacher, Boelcke, but he had learned well and passed the knowledge on to his command. Traveling in packs over the lines they would take a terrible toll of the British planes and pilots.

The year opened badly for the British. On New Year's day, 1917, four new Handley-Page 0/100s, the latest of their heavy bombers (kept a deep secret for a year), took off for France. By mistake one of the pilots landed on a German airfield, thus supplying the enemy with a fine example of the latest English bombing plane. (In the summer of 1916 a similar incident occurred and the Germans received a factory-fresh F.E. 2D even before the British did.) Captured planes were flown and studied by all pilots to learn the plane's weak points as well as its assets and armament.

By April 2, Richthofen had increased his number of "kills" to thirty-four, most of his victims being F.E.s and B.E.s, which were easily outperformed by the Albatros. Included, however, in his 1917 victories were a Sopwith Pup and Strutter, Nieuports and a Spad. It was on April 5 that Richthofen's Jasta 11 set the theme for "Bloody April." That was the day on which the new Bristol Fighter F2A was introduced to the front by No. 48 Squadron under command of William Leefe Robinson, who had destroyed the SL-11 before the eyes of all of London the past September. He was given his command partly as recognition of his exploit. But, other than that night encounter with the wooden German army airship, Leefe Robinson's combat experience was practically nil—and the same was true of the other pilots and observers in his Bristol fighters.

The Bristol was a formidable fighting plane carrying one Vickers machine gun firing through the propeller. In addition, one, or often two, Lewis guns were attached on the Scarff ring in the rear cockpit. It was hoped that this plane would take an important part in the battle over Arras. This offensive, it was hoped, would prove to be the final, decisive one of the war and was to be the British contribution to the great plan of the French general, Robert George Nivelle. The vociferous, energetic Nivelle, a hero of Verdun, had replaced Marshal Joseph Joffre as commander in chief of the Allied armies. Joffre's star had fallen after Verdun (which he had permitted to be stripped of its guns and men) and the Battle of the Somme. Nivelle proposed one massive offensive like "a great blow of a gigantic fist," all along the Western Front in the spring of 1917. He all but guaranteed that it would bring the war to a speedy close.

But Nivelle did not know that the Germans had begun, as early as February 25, to withdraw from the sector facing the British to the heavily fortified Siegfried-Stellung, or as it was to become better known, the Hindenburg Line. The British attack at Arras was but the opening blow of the great offensive and was supposed to distract the Germans from the main attack that Nivelle had planned on the Aisne.

Before the Battle of Arras opened on April 9, 1917, the British planes flew continually over the area, making photographs and attacking enemy

A Handley-Page bomber brought down by the Germans. Among other missions, the 0/400 was dispatched to bomb the bases of Germany's heavy bomber, the Gotha

planes. On that fateful April 5, Leefe Robinson led five other new Bristol fighters on their first patrol over the lines toward Douai. As they approached they could see five Albatros D-IIIs climbing toward them—the lead plane was painted red from spinner to tail.

The British pilots had been instructed not to maneuver the Bristols around too violently in the mistaken belief that they were structurally weak. Therefore, all six planes furnished stable targets for the Albatroses when they attacked. Richthofen accounted for two himself and Leefe Robinson's Bristol fell before the guns of a rookie pilot, Sebastian Festner. The battle lasted about half an hour and of the six Bristols, only two returned to their base, one of them all but demolishing itself upon landing. Leefe Robinson was taken prisoner and, weakened by prison life, died of pneumonia on December 31, 1918.

The Bristol fighter, too, almost suffered a premature end, for the encounter with Jasta 11 almost convinced the British of its inferiority and succeeded in impressing the Germans with its inferiority. This attitude, in time, would cost a great number of German lives.

The day after the battle between Richthofen's Albatros and Leefe Robinson's Brisfits, the Sixty-fifth Congress of the United States of America in a joint resolution declared war upon "the German Imperial Government." Almost two years had passed since the sinking of the *Lusitania*. A complexity of reasons, including a German renewal of unrestricted submarine warfare and Allied atrocity propaganda, had finally led President Woodrow Wilson to ask for the declaration. To the exhausted fighting nations aligned against

The Bristol F2B, the "Brisfit," one of the finest aircraft developed during the war. Capable of speeds in excess of 120-mph and highly maneuverable, the Bristol fighter, a two-seater, carried a Vickers machine gun fixed to fire through the propeller and a flexible Lewis on a Scarff ring at the rear cockpit. Although the Brisfit did not acquit itself very well, principally because its pilots were inexperienced, at the Battle of Arras, it eventually brought an end to "Bloody April"

Germany the news came as the answer to a fervent prayer; but it would be some time before it would be answered in full.

The British were not about to wait until help came from America. To deal with Richthofen's Jasta 11, night bombing was carried out against the airdrome at Douai, although with no great results. In addition, No. 56 Squadron, Maj. R. G. Bloomfield commanding, was organized to deal with the Richthofen *staffel*. With Capt. Albert Ball as his star, Bloomfield carefully chose his other pilots—although he did not attempt to assemble a squadron of aces as had the French in their Cigognes. On the other hand, Bloomfield did select as many good musicians as he could find, often swapping personnel so that his man combined excellent flying and fighting qualities with musical talent. No. 56 Squadron was not only an outstanding fighter unit, it was also an orchestra.

The leading two-seater ace, Major Andrew McKeever, a Canadian who served with No. 11 Squadron, R.F.C. Together with his observer, Sgt. L. F. Powell, McKeever, flying the Bristol fighter, shot down thirty German planes, most of them the dreaded Albatros                    ROYAL CANADIAN AIR FORCE

Albert Ball did not particularly relish his position as flight commander for he was essentially a loner, preferring to hunt on his own rather than lead a group of planes. He was also unhappy with the plane given No. 56 Squadron—the S.E. 5 (Scouting Experimental). Armed with the newly developed Constantinesco hydraulic synchronization gear—as opposed to Fokker's mechanical gear—the S.E. 5 was armed with a single Vickers machine gun mounted on the cowling just in front of the cockpit and firing through the propeller; another gun, a Lewis, was on a Foster mounting atop the wing's center section and was fired by means of a Bowden cable. The S.E. 5 was an excellent fighter although, because of its higher degree of inherent stability (owing in part to the fact that it was powered by an in-line Hispano-Suiza engine and not a revolving rotary), it was not as maneuverable as the Nieuport or the Sopwith Camel. But it was fast and an excellent dogfighter. In time, Ball would come to accept the S.E. 5 as a worthy aircraft (and other British aces—Mannock, Bishop and McCudden—proved its worthiness without question), but in the beginning he frequently wrote to his parents complaining about the plane.

There were, of course—as with all new aircraft rushed into operations—certain deficiencies. Designed as it was by non-fliers of the Royal Aircraft Factory, there were certain aspects of the plane that hindered its primary function. The original windscreen, for example, interfered with the pilot's vision; this defect was subsequently corrected in the field and in later production models, including the later, more powerfully engined S.E. 5A.

Ball returned to France in time to participate in the aerial duels over the Battle of Arras, the first phase of which opened on Easter morning, April 9. Ball led his first patrol, in his S.E. 5 (although he had by then also reacquired a Nieuport), on April 22. The next day he was out on his own in his Nieuport, shot down an Albatros and forced down a German two-seater. By May 6, alternately using both the Nieuport and S.E. 5, to which he had become reconciled, Ball shot down eleven enemy aircraft bringing his total up to 43. Just the day before, he had written to his fiancée in England: "Won't it be nice when all this beastly killing is over, and we can enjoy ourselves and not hurt anyone? I hate this game. . . ."

For Albert Ball, just twenty, the game was practically over. Although he had a roving commission to hunt as he wished, Ball took off with ten other S.E. 5s of No. 56 Squadron in the evening of May 7. The eleven planes were to join two other formations of Spads and Camels in patroling the Cambrai-Douai area on the lookout for the Richthofen Albatros. The weather was threatening and the skies filled with cumulus clouds, great masses of ever-shifting death traps and hiding places for the fighters.

A red Very rocket arched across the face of one of the bloated clouds—a warning signal that the English flight leader had sighted enemy aircraft. The S.E. 5s dropped down upon the unsuspecting German machines, six of them, which suddenly scattered under the attack. Then, from above swooped several red Albatroses of the Richthofen squadron. A confusion of darting and dodging aircraft began tumbling through the sky firing bursts of machine-gun bullets whenever an enemy machine crossed their sights. Soon other German planes, attracted by the melee, joined the fight. So did a flight of British Royal Naval Air Service Sopwith Triplanes. Even so, the British were outnumbered, and although an Albatros could be seen burning on its way to the ground, the losses of the British were higher.

Albert Ball, his plane easily identifiable because of the red spinner he had put on his propeller (he felt it increased the speed; it was also an individual marker not generally permitted by the R.F.C.), was darting in and out of the fight. His squadron mate Cecil Lewis, also busy in the confusing combat,

A new member of the Lafayette Escadrille undergoes inspection. "Soda," the lion cub, mascot of the Lafayette, encircled by James Norman Hall, William Thaw, Dudley Hill, Kenneth Marr, David Peterson, Raoul Lufbery, Robert Rockwell (cousin of Kiffin) and a French officer, Lieutenant Manet. Behind Manet is Ray C. Bridgeman. This photograph was taken in the Aisne sector in 1917

U. S. AIR FORCE

caught the last glimpse of Ball "going east at 8,000 feet. He flew straight into the white face of an enormous cloud. I followed. But when I came out on the other side, he was nowhere to be seen."

Lewis returned to Vert Galand, the base, to learn that of the eleven ships that had gone out only his and four others had returned. Among the missing six was Albert Ball.

There are two stories about how he died, the favored one concerning a secret machine-gun nest in a church tower. It was supposedly Ball's habit when he was returning from a sortie to fly over the church tower in the German-held village of Annoeullin to check his watch. Having noted this, the Germans had only to set a machine gun up in the belfry and wait. According to this legend, once Ball dived through the cloud into which Lewis had seen him go, he dropped down to almost ground level, as was his habit, to check the time on his way back to Vert Galand. As he flashed by the steeple, the machine gun caught him unawares and his S.E. 5 fell on the outskirts of Annoeullin.

A second version, or legend, of how Ball was shot down gives credit for the kill to Lothar von Richthofen, younger brother of the great Baron (who was at the time away from the front on leave). Himself wounded, the younger

142

The funeral of Edmond Charles Genêt, of Ossining, N. Y., a Lafayette Escadrille flier. Genêt was the first American to be killed in aerial combat after the U. S. declared war on Germany. Struck by antiaircraft while on patrol, Genêt fell on April 16, 1917. Other Americans, of course, died before that date, among them Victor Chapman (1916) and Capt. Ely Miller, who borrowed a French Spad and was killed in combat on March 9, 1917. At the time, Miller's squadron, the 95th Aero, was not active so he was not officially serving with the U. S. forces. Neither, for that matter, was Genêt. He is still regarded as the first American to fall after the U. S. declaration of war          U. S. AIR FORCE

Richthofen claimed an aircraft shot down, although initially he described it as a triplane (which might have been one of the naval aircraft from No. 6 Squadron, which had engaged in the fight also). Although, in time, the Germans claimed that Lothar von Richthofen had killed Albert Ball, it appears to be an *ex post facto* decision. Lothar could not give a coherent account of his victory—he had become lost in flight and was wounded seriously enough to faint upon landing.

That Albert Ball crashed just outside Annoeullin is definite. His body was badly battered (although a British prisoner of war was able to identify it— three weeks after), his cigarette case was found and his wallet contained clippings about himself from Nottingham newspapers. For a time it was suggested that Ball had been hit by antiaircraft fire. But the Germans considered it good propaganda to credit the kill to a von Richthofen instead.

Whatever occurred on the evening of May 7, 1917, the fate of young Capt. Albert Ball has never been resolved and continues to be argued about among

The excellent S.E. 5 ("Scouting Experimental") fighter, although not as maneuverable as the rotary-powered Camel, the S.E. 5 handled as well and was capable of taking structural strain of combat. The S.E. 5 (as well as the Camel) replaced the Nieuports with which many British units were equipped in early 1917

the various "experts," each with his pet theory. Some would not credit a mere ground gunner with the ability to kill Ball, others place Lothar von Richthofen in a hospital on the day of the actual encounter; few would admit to a lucky antiaircraft hit. No one seems to consider the possibility that an unknown German pilot, himself killed in the same combat, might have shot Ball down and could never make the claim. Even more ignored by the romantics is the fact that to the not yet twenty-one-year-old British ace, the means made no difference at all; the end had come to the killing he detested, and the future he had hoped for—marriage and in some business or other in Nottingham—would never be.

By curious coincidence, on the very day Ball was killed, another British flier, newly posted with No. 40 Squadron and flying the Nieuport fighter, scored his first aerial victory over a German balloon. His name was Edward Mannock. He was Ball's opposite, proving himself as time went by to be an outstanding flight commander, a cool and calculating tactician, and one of the few airmen who harbored a truly burning hatred for the Germans. No knightly jouster he.

The Sopwith F. 1 "Camel," the nickname derived from the humplike cowling on the upper forward fuselage over the twin Vickers machine guns. The Camel, because of its rotary engine, was a tricky plane to fly. One pilot, Norman MacMillan, wrote of the plane, "The Camel was a fierce little beast. She answered readily to intelligent handling, but she was utterly remorseless against brutal or ignorant treatment." Because of the whirling engine in the nose, the Camel turned very quickly to the right, a maneuver which confused German pilots as well as inexperienced British pilots. For the former it meant death in combat; for the latter it meant death in a training accident     JARRETT COLLECTION

Mannock had been the pupil of James McCudden during the latter's occasional absences from the fighting front. The era of the roving commission was practically over; to fight with the formations of the Richthofen "Flying Circus," as the gaily colored planes were being called by the British, it was necessary to fight back in formation also. The individual fell quickly to a pack; the team idea had finally come into its own, later to evolve into the incipient leader and wingman concept which would prove so effective during World War II.

Possibly one of the last of the British individualists was the Canadian, William Avery Bishop, who had by May 1917 shot down seven enemy aircraft, including one balloon in only about two months of combat flying.

Although the French High Command also favored formation flying, they could not interfere with the style of their adored hero George Guynemer, whose end was to be an extraordinary sequel to Albert Ball's. The hold of this tall, slender and spoiled young man upon the French people is indescrib-

145

able. His mail was filled with letters from girls and women proposing marriage; schoolchildren requested his autograph. He was followed in the streets, and when his Spad was placed on display in Paris, flowers were placed around it by a loving population. Neither Ferdinand Foch, hero of the Marne, nor Henri Philippe Pétain, "Saviour of Verdun," enjoyed such an outpouring of love. But neither were they consumptive twenty-two-year-olds with the grace and carriage of a girl who engaged in single combat with the Boche. Even more curious was the admiration for him displayed by the lowly *poilu,* the common, anonymous and suffering French foot soldier who envied and even resented the soft and highly publicized life of the aces.

In a characteristic letter to his father, Guynemer reported a typical day for him, except for its near-tragic conclusion:

> September 23: 11:20—A Boche in flames within our lines. 11:21—A Boche disabled, passenger killed. 11:25—A Boche in flames 400 meters from the lines. 11:25½—A [French] 75 blew up my water reservoir, and all the linen of the left upper plane [wing], hence a superb tailspin. Succeeded in changing it into a glide. Fell to ground at speed of 160-

The end of "Bloody April"—an Albatros after having crashed to the ground

Lothar von Richthofen, brother of the German ace of aces. At the war's end the younger Richthofen's score stood at forty, just half that of his famous brother's. Lothar claimed credit for shooting down of British ace Albert Ball, but it was never actually proved. More affable than the "Red Knight," his brother, Lothar von Richthofen was a popular pilot in Jasta 11          JARRETT COLLECTION

> 180 kilometers: everything broken like matches, then the "taxi" rebounded, turned around at 45 degrees, and came back, head down, planting itself in the ground 40 meters away like a post; they could not budge it. Nothing was left but the body, which was intact: the Spad is strong; with any other machine I should now be thinner than this sheet of paper.

Guynemer had dropped almost 10,000 feet at high speed in a disabled Spad shot down by his own artillerymen. He actually struck the earth *before* his last victim—the 11:25 Boche—crashed. When the French infantrymen rushed out to the wingless Spad, which had dug itself into the ground, they expected to pull the broken pilot out of the wreckage. Instead, a slender, pale figure with enormous black eyes and just the suggestion of a wispy mustache stood up. Guynemer! The soldiers bore him off to their position, where the division commander, a general, commanded a salute for the great Guynemer.

"You will review the troops with me," he told the shaken flyer.

"I happen to be wounded, General."

"Wounded—you! Impossible!"

But it was possible, for Guynemer had a badly gashed knee and was suffering from concussion. But he stood, leaning upon the general, while the troops marched past. Then spontaneously someone began the strains of the "Marseillaise" and soon the air in the sector rang with the voices of men, even those in the trenches, singing a tribute to their beloved knight of the air.

147

Georges Guynemer, an official portrait. When this photo was taken, the youthful
Guynemer was attempting to grow a mustache        JARRETT COLLECTION

That was but one of the seven times Guynemer was shot down and survived. Over Verdun he fell under the guns of five German planes, with a
badly wounded arm which forced him to return to his home at Compiègne to
recuperate. Although he was not required to fly, was not supposed to in fact,
Guynemer arranged to have his Nieuport sent to a nearby airdrome. His sister
Yvonne promised to keep an eye on the weather and to inform him when it
was favorable for flight.

One morning in the spring of 1916, when his wounds had healed sufficiently to enable him to fly and Yvonne had informed him that the weather
was fine, Guynemer left the family house on a strange mission. When he returned, his sister was still in bed and the day had barely dawned. Guynemer
then told her what he had done.

To test his nerve, for it was believed that a wound could adversely affect a
pilot, Guynemer flew over the lines and literally played with a German plane.

148

A portrait by J. C. Lawrence showing Guynemer checking the guns of his Spad before taking off. The expression and the cast of Guynemer's eyes were recognized by his squadron mates as signs of the French ace's urge to kill. This expression came upon him as he prepared to go into combat          JARRETT COLLECTION

Flying directly at the enemy without firing a single shot, Guynemer darted around the puzzled German, weaving and dodging. Finally, after the German had expended 500 rounds without hitting him, and Guynemer was convinced that his nerves were as steel-like as ever, he returned home. A deadly shot, he could very easily have gunned down the German plane but permitted it to return. "That," he later said, "was the decisive moment of my life."

It is impossible to remove the great cloud of myth and romanticism enveloping Guynemer, or to know what demon drove him. He was genuinely patriotic and killed the enemies of France with pleasure. That another human being perished in flames before his eyes—on one occasion he saw both passengers leap from a plane he had set aflame and fall thousands of feet—did

149

Guynemer in his Spad, *Vieux Charles*. Note special windscreen around the cockpit and the rearview mirror on upper wing

not seem to bother him. His delicate physical condition which, from time to time, necessitated his withdrawing from active duty for hospitalization, may have been a factor. The senior Guynemer had been a soldier, although he had not passed any of his physical power onto his son. Young Georges, coddled and petted by two older sisters and his mother, had proved so delicate a child that he did not attend school with other children until he was twelve.

When war came he was chagrined to be turned down twice when he volunteered for duty. Even as a youngster Guynemer revealed a marked scientific bent and mechanical ability; these skills, plus his father's influence, helped him into the Air Service. Resented at first as a rich man's son and a weakling, Guynemer quickly proved himself a superior mechanic and a willing hard worker. He was also persistent and talked his way into the flying branch of the Air Service.

The machine compensated for his own physical limitations; it became quite literally the extension of himself. Guynemer understood his planes, his guns, his ammunition, as well as he understood himself. On the ground, he was moody, diffident and rarely in good health. In the air he was terror itself; his friend and biographer Henri Bordeaux described this transformation almost in terms of a seizure, as if Guynemer's personality changed just before he took off in his fighter. His face became deathly pale and his eyes flashed with a strange light. "He carried fire and massacre up into the sky," Bordeaux concluded.

150

The French Spad—the name derived from the initials S.P.A.D., *Société Pour Aviation et ses Dérivés*. The Spad, unlike the Nieuport, was an extremely rugged aircraft, could take unlimited manhandling and could pull out of power dives without disintegrating. Flying it also took skill, for it lacked inherent stability (i.e., it did not fly itself as did other planes) and did not glide very well, necessitating a rather high landing speed. The Spad was used by French, British and American pilots. It was an especial favorite of the latter     U. S. AIR FORCE

Excellent marksmanship, skillful pilotage and an indefinable demon combined to make Guynemer a killer in the air, a killer who did not seem to mind too much the idea of being killed himself. For all his skill, he was an impetuous air fighter rather than a scientific one. He was concerned primarily with ridding the skies of his personal enemies, the enemies of his beloved France; the large dimension—the Great War—was no great concern of his.

On May 25, 1917, Guynemer made history along the front when he shot down four enemy aircraft in one day, two of them within one minute of each other. He was hailed in France as *as des as,* the "ace of aces." In recognition of this feat he was awarded the badge of an Officer in the Legion of Honor; but before the ceremony, Guynemer had completed two patrols, attacked an enemy two-seater and returned with five bullets in his engine and radiator.

The pace was telling; physically and mentally Guynemer was paying the price. The adoration of the crowds did not impress him; when he could not fly he was restless. He spent much of his time, when he could not fly because of weather or health, either visiting the Spad factories or writing to the de-

151

Guynemer's French identification card as it appeared when published in the German magazine *Die Woche*, after the French ace's disappearance. It was all that was taken from his body before Guynemer and his Spad were demolished by artillery fire                                    JARRETT COLLECTION

signer Louis Béchereau. Guynemer had definite ideas, as had Albert Ball, on the qualities that made for an excellent fighter machine. One of his ideas was called "The Magic Machine," a Spad armed with a cannon which fired through the hollow propeller shaft. The weapon was a 37 mm single-shot cannon, which proved somewhat impractical. Unless Guynemer hit with the first shot, he would have to spend much valuable time reloading the gun before it could be fired again. Also, the fumes from the gun filled the cockpit, nauseating him; another problem was the gun's recoil, which did very little good to the Spad's airframe.

In spite of the handicaps Guynemer actually shot down planes while flying his "Magic Machine," an idea which was ahead of its time and was used in World War II.

When he was not somehow occupied, Guynemer was unhappy. He refused to take a rest, and even after his victory list reached the remarkable score of 50, he refused to retire from combat to serve as an instructor. He did not like to have any mention made of his future. "Do not let us make any plans," he would snap. Or he would look back upon his combat career and gloomily observe, "I have been too lucky and I feel as if I must pay for it."

During World War II, a flight surgeon would have grounded any pilot who spoke in this manner. But there was no grounding the immortal Guynemer, who pretty much had his own way, deferred to as he was by his superiors and the object of love by all others.

In September 1917, Herteaux, who commanded the Cignognes (the Stork Squadron), was wounded and Guynemer was appointed in his place. He did not like command, the demands of desk work annoyed him, and he sought relief in the air. He found no consolation in his promotion to the rank of Captain. Shortly after, on Tuesday, September 11, the final touch was applied to the Guynemer legend. The morning had been foggy, but the sun had burned that off. Impatient, Guynemer had prowled about the base; in one of the sheds he inspected his Spad *Vieux-Charles,* which had suffered jammed machine guns the day before and a defect in the water pump. These had apparently been cleared up to Guynemer's satisfaction. He decided not to wait around until the arrival of his old commander, Brocard. The latter had been summoned by some of Guynemer's squadron who were worried over the health of the ace of aces, hoping that Brocard might be able to talk him into taking a rest.

In the company of a young lieutenant, Benjamen Bozon-Verduraz, Guynemer took off shortly after 8 o'clock. Brocard had wired that he would arrive around nine—they would be back in time to meet him. They were over Poelcapelle, northwest of Ypres, Belgium, when Guynemer signaled to Bozon-Verduraz that he had sighted an enemy plane, a two-seater Aviatik. He dived in to attack while his companion searched the skies for other planes.

Guynemer apparently missed on his first pass and turned to make another. The German plane dropped into an evasive spin and Guynemer followed. Bozon-Verduraz saw eight German single-seaters and went into action, hoping to draw them away from Guynemer. The formation broke up but no real battle ensued, and Bozon-Verduraz returned to the spot where he had last seen Guynemer diving after the Aviatik.

The sky was empty. The lieutenant then swooped down near the ground and searched, relieved to find no wreckage there. He returned to the sky again and continued flying until his fuel became dangerously low and then returned to his base. Guynemer had not returned. A deep gloom fell upon the airdrome; by nightfall it was obvious that something had happened to Guynemer.

But what? There was no announcement from the Germans—who would certainly have noted the capture or death of so celebrated a man. The French made no announcement either. Finally the news leaked and was published in a London paper on September 17. Then German claims were made, assigning the honor of knocking down the French *as des as* to one Lt. Kurt Wissemann of Jagdstaffel No. 3, although he claimed to have done this on September 10, the day before Guynemer had disappeared.

The mystery of Guynemer's conqueror was never resolved although his fate was obvious—and, in fact, was reported through the Spanish Embassy by the German Foreign Office. In his battle with the Aviatik, Guynemer may have been hit by the gunner, for his Spad crashed near a graveyard just south of Poelcapelle. He had been shot through the head, a German physician had

René Paul Fonck, the French, as well as Allied, ace of aces at the war's end. Unlike Guynemer and Nungesser, Fonck was a careful tactician and did not practice the headlong attack style. Fonck's official total was 75

found, the forefinger of his left hand had been shot away and a leg had been broken in the crash. The investigation by the surgeon and two soldiers was carried out under difficult conditions, for the area was under attack (some of the witnesses to the crash were killed in this attack) and before the body could be removed from the plane, or even buried, the area had to be evacuated under artillery fire. The British guns then obliterated all traces of Guynemer and his Spad. There seems little reason to discredit this version of Guynemer's end, although the French at the time simply could not accept it. The nation was plunged into mourning for their beloved knight of the air, whose death made a deeper impression upon the national consciousness than the thousands occurring every day on the Western Front.

The October 6, 1917, issue of *L'Illustration* expressed the final word on the subject:

He was neither seen nor heard as he fell, his body and his machine were never found. Where has he gone? By what wings did he manage to glide into immortality? Nobody knows: nothing is known. He ascended and never came back, that is all. Perhaps our descendents will say: "He flew so high that he could not come down again."

In more than 600 combats (665 hours and 55 minutes, according to his own log) George Guynemer had shot down 54 enemy aircraft. The legend that "he flew so high that he could not come down again" persists among French schoolchildren to this day.

No other French airman was ever to fill the void left by the disappearance of Guynemer—although his place as *as des as* was taken over by meticulous

Charles Eugène Jules Marie Nungesser, third-ranking French ace with 45 enemy aircraft to his credit. In this formal portrait Nungesser, fully bemedaled, displays little of the punishment he absorbed while fighting for France. Scars, however, may be seen on his chin and over his left eye. It is said that Nungesser actually flew into combat wearing his medals          FRENCH EMBASSY

Manfred von Richthofen about to board his private transport, a two-seater which was furnished complete with pilot. In this ship Richthofen flew from the front to meet with German dignitaries, to enjoy a leave devoted to hunting, or to visit his family. Kurt Wolff stands to Richthofen's left

René Paul Fonck, whose official score of kills on November 11, 1918, would reach 75; Guynemer was second on the official list of aces with a total of 54. Nungesser, who like Fonck, survived, had 45. Next in line was Capt. Georges Felix Madon (41) and Lt. Michel Coiffard (34). Lt. Jean Pierre Leon Bourjade, who had been studying for the priesthood when the war began, proved himself to be an outstanding destroyer of balloons. He ended the war with a total of 24 balloons and 4 aircraft to his credit. He then returned to his religious training and died in the tropics while ministering to lepers. Armand Pinsard was next on the list with 27 victories, followed by René Dorme, (23 victories). Dorme, like Guynemer, had been a member of the Storks, the best known of all French escadrilles.

Richthofen and the German Empress, wife of the Kaiser    JARRETT COLLECTION

Richthofen meeting with Kaiser Wilhelm in Flanders, August 1917
JARRETT COLLECTION

Dorme, who was close to Guynemer, had earned the nickname of "Père" because of his paternal concern for the other Storks. Although of a sunnier disposition and a less complex personality than Guynemer, Dorme shared with him a deep love for France. Inside his Nieuport he carried a mascot, a small doll dressed in the native costume of his native province, Lorraine. Dorme fell in flames on the same day that Guynemer made history by shooting down four enemy aircraft. The loss of "Père" Dorme tarnished the gold of Guynemer's accomplishment and he sadly recalled Dorme, commenting that his "uprightness, artlessness and kindness made him beloved of all. Of a steel-like energy, he was gentleness itself." The final sentence could very aptly serve as Guynemer's epitaph—although a much longer one was cut into the Pantheon in Paris.

The Germans too were losing their airmen. Later, when they looked back, the fliers realized that they had sensed a change in the air war during 1917. The sport had become deadly, and years of inconclusive, depleting, ground warfare had brought a sense of desperate urgency to the fighting.

Richthofen's Jasta 11, the "Flying Circus," lined up at Douai, France, just before the March offensive. Richthofen's Albatros is the second one from the front, without German Cross on tail and with a ladder beside it. The ladder was used to get into the cockpit when encumbered with heavy flying clothes    JARRETT COLLECTION

The superiority of the Albatros and Halberstadt planes, which had made "Bloody April" a grim month for the British, waned with the wider introduction of the S.E. 5s, Camels and the Spad. Von Richthofen's Jasta 11, although not the only fighter squadron on the front, was the star unit, and by the end of April had one hundred British planes to its credit. And while the leader was the outstanding member, others were attracting notice also. One was Kurt Wolff, who on April 29, 1917, shot down Maj. H.D. Harvey-Kelly, the first British pilot to land in France when the war began. Wolff sent Harvey-Kelly's Spad down in flames. In the same dogfight Richthofen also shot down a Spad piloted by Lt. R. Applin, bringing his victory total up to 49; his brother Lothar also scored and his score numbered nineteen.

But April ended and Manfred von Richthofen was called away to an audiance with the Kaiser, who wished to meet the hero of Germany. Lothar von Richthofen was left in charge of the squadron. His older brother, even before he went home to be with his family, set out for the Black Forest to hunt. He planned to stay away for weeks, not returning until mid-June. On June

General Erich von Ludendorff visits the Flying Circus at Marcke in August 1917

26 he received orders to group Jastas 4, 6, 10 and 11 into Jagdgeschwader Nr. 1, which he would command. His orders directed Richthofen to "attain air supremacy in sectors of the front as directed." Instead of being stationed permanently at one base, Richthofen and his J. G. 1 could be moved along the front to those sections when the need arose. Thus was Richthofen's "Flying Circus" born; the gaily colored aircraft became familiar along the Western Front.

Richthofen placed Kurt Wolff at the head of his own Jasta 11. There was some sadness mingled with the excitement of the reorganizations, for on June 27 Leutnant Karl Allmenröder of Jasta 11 was shot down by a pilot in a Royal Naval Air Service Sopwith Triplane. He was the Canadian Raymond Collishaw, commander of "B" flight, No. 10 (Naval) Squadron. Collishaw was the leader of the famed "Black Flight," all Canadian pilots in grimly darkened Sopwith Triplanes (which had not impressed the R.F.C. but went to the R.N.A.S. and served very well). Collishaw's plane was named *Black Maria,* the others in his flight being named *Black Death, Black Prince, Black Roger* and *Black Sheep.* It was one of the most potent fighting units of the war.

Allmenröder, one of the original members of Jasta 11, had only received the *Pour le Mérite* and had a total of 30 victories to his credit. Richthofen had planned to place him in command of one of his Jastas. Barely had he begun to settle down in his new position when Richthofen himself was shot down.

159

On July 6, Richthofen had led a patrol and encountered a formation of old F.E. 2ds of No. 20 Squadron. Outclassed by the Germans in their Albatros fighters, the F.E.s formed into a circle, so that the gunner in the front cockpit could cover the plane in front of him. Thus circling and bristling, the English two-seaters gradually edged back to the English lines. Any attempt by a German plane to attack would be met by a withering fire from one gun or another in the circle of F.E.s. From one of them, piloted by Capt. D. C. Cunnell, Lt. A. E. Woodbridge fired at an all-red Albatros D-V.

From one of the German observation posts on the ground Hans Schröder watched the strange fight. It was his duty to warn the German airdromes of the approach of Allied aircraft. Then to his horror he saw an Albatros, which he recognized as Richthofen's, suddenly drop out of the battle. The plane was plunging vertically for the ground. At around 500 feet, it pulled out faltered and continued down. With his telescope Schröder could see two of Richthofen's squadron mates circling over the spot where the Albatros had fallen.

Schröder left his post and ran nearly a mile to the crash and there found Richthofen out of his wrecked plane, his face white and his head covered with blood. Removing Richthofen's flying helmet, Schröder applied a field bandage and ordered an ambulance. For this action he was almost court-martialed for leaving his post; only the intervention of Richthofen prevented it.

What had happened was that Woodbridge's long shot had grazed Richthofen's skull, which caused him to lose consciousness until he was about 500 feet from the ground. Although in shock and half-fainting Richthofen realized through the fog that he must pull the Albatros out of the death dive. He managed to do that, but blacked out again, came to and crash-landed the plane. It had not burned (probably because he had the presence of mind to turn off the ignition), and he struggled out of the cockpit and fell to the ground where, out of breath, Schröder had found him. He would be out of combat for a month, and the belief is that after he had returned, Richthofen was never the same. He had lost some of his spirit.

By the time he rejoined his Circus, the new Fokker Triplane was introduced. Fokker had gone into comparative eclipse following the brief heyday of the Fokker E series. Denied access to the in-line Oberursal engines such as were being used on the Albatros and Halberstadt, Fokker had to get around German political intrigue by turning out aircraft which could use the more easily obtained rotaries. His early biplanes, the "D" series, though purchased by the German air force, were not widely used and generally relegated to the quieter fronts.

With the triplane, more officially "Dr I"—which was introduced after the British Sopwith Triplanes had been in service for several months—Fokker again became a name to be reckoned with along the Western Front. It was, incidentally, designed by Reinhold Platz—a fact Fokker himself generally neglected to mention.

Raymond Collishaw, the Canadian who was to become third-ranking British ace. An exponent of the Sopwith Triplane, Collishaw later commanded No. 13 Naval Squadron which was outfitted with Camels. In the cockpit of this Camel is Captain At. Whealey. Collishaw shot down sixty German planes and lived to serve also in the Second World War as an air vice-marshal in the R.A.F.

ROYAL CANADIAN AIR FORCE

There had been some dissatisfaction with the Albatros which, though fast, evidenced structural failure on occasion often resulting in death for German fliers. The Triplane, which was certainly one of the most striking-looking aircraft of World War I, was slower than the Albatros, but was exceptionally maneuverable owing to its stubby wings. With his usual political acumen, Fokker presented the first production models to von Richthofen's Geschwader, the first going to the Baron himself and the second to twenty-year-old Werner Voss.

When Richthofen went on leave again in September (he was not yet completely recovered from his wound), his Triplane was taken over by Oberleutnant Kurt Wolff, who led four Albatros D-Vs on a patrol. The Triplane

Richthofen in the hospital after being wounded in July 1917    JARRETT COLLECTION

Nurse Kätie Otersdorf and her patient, Baron Manfred von Richthofen, while he was recuperating at the St. Nicholas hospital at Courtrai    JARRETT COLLECTION

became separated from the Albatroses over Wervicq, and while Wolff was alone, he was attacked by a patrol of British Camels from No. 10 Naval Squadron. Even as the Albatroses raced to the fight, Wolff's Fokker was seen to break into a spin, flames shooting from the engine. There was an explosion and only small pieces continued falling to the ground. The leader of Jasta 11 joined the other fatalities of the Richthofen Circus.

The youthful Werner Voss, whom Richthofen had chosen to command Jasta 10 of the Circus, was the champion of the Fokker Triplane. Despite this, and the fact that Richthofen also liked the plane, it was not quite the outstanding craft that it has now come to be believed. Nor was it the favorite of many German pilots. But Voss liked it and proved, even before Richthofen, the craft's capabilities. At the time, Voss was Germany's second-ranking ace, second only to the great Red Knight himself. His fighting style was much like that of Albert Ball, who also had been an ace before he was twenty, and Guynemer—a style, which by mid-1917, had few advocates, especially among German pilots. Undoubtedly Voss's youth had much to do

162

A visitor, Oberleutnant W. Reinhard (who later succeeded Richthofen as commander of the Flying Circus). The Red Knight wears his Pour le Mérite around his neck                JARRETT COLLECTION

with his fighting style. He was also a superb pilot, so skilled that he was at first assigned as an instructor on completing his flying instruction. (Like so many other top World War I fliers, Voss originally served in the cavalry at the war's outbreak.)

The Fokker Triplane fascinated Voss; this led to the replacement of the Albatros fighters of Jasta 10 with triplanes, which he preferred to either the Albatros or the Pfalz (originally intended as a replacement for the Albatros and Halberstadt scouts, but outclassed by the Fokker).

By the end of September, Voss had raised his score to forty-eight, just thirteen behind Richthofen. It was on September 23 that Voss, flying his silvery-blue triplane, encountered "B" Flight of No. 56 Squadron, R.F.C. Voss had attacked a single S.E. 5 which attracted the six S.E. 5As of No. 56 led by Capt. James McCudden. The single S.E. 5 seemed to be in serious trouble so "B" Flight attacked the lone triplane. Instead of breaking for his own lines, Voss chose to take on the entire British flight. "By now the German triplane was in the middle of our formation," McCudden reported, "and its handling was wonderful to behold."

For at least ten minutes Voss successfully parried with the British aces, darting about the sky like a crazed butterfly. Not one ship in "B" Flight returned that day without the marks of Voss's guns. There were times when he seemed caught in crossfire from several guns, but somehow Voss continued

163

The Fokker triplane of August 1917. Though not fast, the triplane was highly maneuverable (because of its stubby wings and rotary engine) and could dazzle enemy fighter pilots with its unexpected movements in the air. Its major defects were a tendency to shed fabric off the upper wing in a dive and to crumple up in the air under stress of combat. It took a good pilot to fly a triplane

to elude them. For a moment it seemed, too, that he would receive help from a formation of Albatros fighters which had come upon the unequal battle, but only one of the ten remained and he was quickly shot down.

Lt. A. P. F. Rhys-Davids used up two drums of ammunition without any apparent results. Then he got on the tail of the triplane and scored with his forward-firing Vickers. The Fokker no longer made any attempt to evade its pursuers and proceeded to lose altitude in a shallow dive. Rhys-Davids lost track of the plane in the clouds, but McCudden saw it nose down and dive for the ground at about a thousand feet. "As long as I live," McCudden wrote later, "I shall never forget my admiration for that German pilot who single-handed fought seven of us ["B" flight plus the first S.E. 5] for ten minutes, and also put some bullets through all of our machines. His flying was wonderful, his courage magnificent, and in my opinion he is the bravest German airman whom it has been my privilege to see fight."

Kurt Wolff, whom Richthofen had chosen to lead his own Jasta 11 when he became commander of Jagdeschwader (Group) Number 1. Wolff died, however, in Richthofen's Fokker triplane          JARRETT COLLECTION

Werner Voss, champion of the Fokker triplane in which he shot down 22 British planes in 21 days. Voss commanded Jasta 10, one of the first German units to fly the triplane extensively. Voss was killed in combat with British planes in September 1917; at the time he was barely twenty years old     JARRETT COLLECTION

When it was learned that the pilot was the great Werner Voss, Rhys-Davids received many congratulations for his victory, but he confided to McCudden: ". . .if I could only have brought him down alive!"

For a time No. 56 Squadron had been withdrawn from France, prior to its fight with Werner Voss. As the No. 1 fighter unit, it was called back to England to deal with the serious threat of the Gotha, which had come to replace the Zeppelin terror. The airships had proved vulnerable and not as effective as the German High Command had hoped. Only the stubbornness of Strasser, and his inability to realize the limitations of the military airship, kept the German Naval Air Service airships in operation. But by the summer of 1917 it was "Gotha" that became the dreaded word—and a word that was applied to all heavy German bombers.

Heavy Bomber Squadron No. 3—the Englandgeschwader—under command of Capt. E. von Brandenburg, was established specifically to bring the war to the English people where the Zeppelins had failed. The Gotha raids

165

The Gotha Bomber, product of the Gothaer Waggonfabrik, Berlin. It was hoped that the heavy bomber would succeed where the Zeppelin had failed. The later models of the Gotha had a wingspan of 77 feet, 8 inches, and was 40 feet, 9 inches long. Although the bombing of England by the Gothas and the "Giants" did not prove decisive, they did cause more damage and kill more people than did the Zeppelins                                                                              U. S. AIR FORCE

divided up into two phases. The first beginning on May 25, 1917 and running through August 22, was devoted to daylight bombing. Following rather heavy losses to the Gothas, Brandenburg decided to concentrate on night raids.

London—the favorite target of all German commanders—was hit for the first time by the Gothas on June 13; the toll was very high compared to that of the Zeppelins. Over four tons of explosives were dropped on the British capital (126 bombs), killing 162 and injuring 432. The old B.E. 2cs assigned to Home Defence squadrons were ineffective and it was at this point that No. 56 Squadron was recalled from France to be based near London; No. 66 Squadron (flying Sopwith Pups) was stationed near Calais. The Gotha campaign might have been judged reasonably effective even at this early stage, for it involved two first-line fighter squadrons in rather futile defense measures when they might have been better employed in France.

The Gotha raids slackened by early July—London especially was left alone, on July 5, however, the Naval Air Station at Felixstowe was bombed —there were 47 casualties and a flying boat was destroyed.

A squadron of Gothas line up before takeoff to bomb England

The next day, Nos. 56 and 66 Squadrons were ordered back to France, and the day after, (July 7), the Gothas returned to London. Fifty-four Londoners were killed and 190 injured. It was soon obvious that British defense measures were becoming more aggressive and accounted for a Gotha from time to time; the July 7 raid, therefore, was the last daylight attack by the Gothas on London. On one occasion the returning bombers were intercepted by James McCudden, who emptied his guns into a big German bomber but was not successful in bringing it down. He followed his intended victim out over the English Channel, hoping he could keep its gunners busy while other British planes moved in for the kill. When his windscreen was shattered in his face by a burst from the Gotha, McCudden (who had no ammunition), low on gas, returned to his base.

Hit-and-run daylight raids continued, but London was only visited by the Gothas at night. On these night raids the Gothas were occasionally accom-

167

London under Gotha attack; fires caused by bombs may be seen scattered around the attack area. This photo was taken from a German bomber    U. S. AIR FORCE

panied by the Giants, bombers which were even larger than the 77-foot-wingspan Gotha. The "Giants," among them such aircraft as the Staaken R-VIs, the A.E.G. and Linke-Hofmann, were powered by four and even six engines. The "R" classification stood for *Riesenflugzeug* ("giant aircraft"), the most successful of which were the Staakens by the Zeppelin company. These were the largest planes of World War I (the span of the Staaken R-VI measured more than 138 feet), carried heavier bombloads than the Gothas, although their very giantism was a liability. They were underpowered, not maneuverable, and the entire program was plagued by accidents. Once again an idea was put forth that would not reach its full, and terrible, fruition until the Second World War's strategic bombardment by giant aircraft—the B-17s, B-24s, the British Lancasters and the ultimate heavy bomber, the B-29.

The strangest Zeppelin raid, and one of the most disastrous for Strasser's naval airships of 1917, occurred on October 19. It was popularly called "The Silent Raid" because the airships, attacking from an altitude of 12,000 feet, were not heard on the ground. Of the eleven airships that crossed over the North Sea to attack industrial targets in the Midlands, four would never return. It was the last airship raid of any size, of the war but not a successful one. Only the veteran von Buttlar, in the L-54, chose to abandon the attack

168

An A.E.G. bomber, another Giant. Note four-wheeled undercarriage and machine gun in front cockpit. A bomb may be seen slung under the fuselage. The A.E.G. (Allgemeine Elektrizitats Gesellschaft), though widely used, was not very good

One of the German Giants, a Siemens-Schuckert bomber. The plane was powered by four engines, two pushers and two tractors. Its very size proved its undoing, for it was difficult to maneuver. The wingspan measured 123 feet

on the Midlands. He went down to 5,000 feet, dropped his bombs and returned to the base at Tondern.

The other ships, gale-driven in the high altitudes, were scattered all over the sky. The L-45 bombed London after spotting the Thames (no searchlights or antiaircraft were in evidence) and bombs fell, seemingly out of an empty, silent sky. Thirty-three people died in London, and fifty were injured, on the night of the Silent Raid. The cost to the attacking force, however, was prohibitive: four airships—the L-44, L-45, L-49 and L-50 were lost—the first was shot down by French A.A. guns, and the others were victims of the high winds. The L-49 came down almost without any damage near Bourbonne-les-Bains in France. French peasants prevented commander Hans-Karl Gayer from destroying the great airship and the Allies had an intact Zeppelin, complete with equipment and documents.

Late in November, the British opened the Battle of Cambrai in which they used tanks effectively for the first time; the advantage thus gained, however, was lost because there were no tanks and infantry in reserve to exploit the opportunity. The Americans who had begun to arrive in France in June, led by Maj. Gen. John J. Pershing, were refreshingly and encouragingly eager, spoiling for a fight and full of fresh, young blood. The French were depleted; after the failure of Nivelle's great offensive, entire units of French troops mutinied. The British were mired in Flanders and the Germans were apprehensive. Plans were hurriedly drawn up to unleash a big German offensive before the Americans were ready.

It was hoped by the Allies that the fresh troops coming from the United States might replace the Russians, who were already discussing surrender plans with the Germans. With the Russians out of the war, the Germans could withdraw the troops from the Eastern Front and concentrate them in the west to oppose the dispirited French and the exhausted British. If the blow could fall before the Americans arrived, the German High Command was certain the war could end in victory for Germany. The mood was one of bitter desperation as a race to launch the big offensive ensued. On the ground the action was still circumscribed by the barbed wire of the trenches.

In the air, as both sides prepared their finest aircraft for the battle to come, the day of the aces had practically ended.

The German Zeppelin L-49 in France following the so-called "Silent Raid" on England, October 20, 1917. At the mercy of high winds in the upper altitudes, the L-49 was blown over France where it fell—after being attacked by five French Nieuports—in the vicinity of Bourbonne-les-Bains. It was captured intact

U. S. AIR FORCE

171

Dogfight: Fokker D-VIIs and S.E. 5s battle over the British lines

# 1918

*There won't be any after-the-war for a fighter pilot.*

—RAOUL LUFBERY

A Fokker disintegrates after an attack by a British S.E. 5
COCKBURN-LANGE PHOTO: JARRETT COLLECTION

# *Air power*

as a serious military concept came of age in 1918. So did the aircraft: the leap in performance from the 66 mph Blériot of 1914 to the 130 mph Spad of 1918 was only a single example of the great technical advances accelerated by the war. Engines and armament had also improved. So had the understanding of the theoretical use of air power—the roving commission of the lone fighter was finished. Formation flying was the key to effective striking power and also mutual protection. The result, when enemy formations met, was air battles on a large scale involving literally dozens—sometimes hundreds—of planes. These were, of course, the classic dogfights chronicled in postwar movies and in the pages of pulp magazines.

Writers have attempted to define a dogfight to fit the grandiose air battles which closed the war (one writer even going so far as to set up specific conditions pertaining to the number of aircraft involved and the amount of sky in which they fought). To the pilots who fought in them, a dogfight was an air battle involving at least two aircraft—and no one bothered about measuring the arena.

Formation tactics and more modern planes did not eliminate the individualist, however. Airmen still looked upon themselves as a breed apart and the more nonconformist among them left their mark on the history of the first war in the air, if not among those who contributed to the actual shortening of the war.

A maverick who left a formation to seek individual combat endangered himself and the formation he had deserted; he also placed the mission of the flight in jeopardy. Fighters—or scouts as they were called—were detailed to escort bombers and to protect them from enemy scouts; or they were sent out to patrol a specific portion of the front, keeping it clear of enemy observation planes—any enemy planes, in fact—to screen the activities on the ground which, if seen, would reveal the plans of the ground forces. Any pilot who dashed off to engage in the sporting duel in no way contributed to the success of the mission. The flight leader would decide when the moment for attack came, if it came at all. If enemy aircraft were sighted they were not necessarily attacked unless it was important to the mission of the patrol. To some pilots the black crosses on the German planes were equivalent to a red flag; if they could not fight, it seemed a waste of time.

While men and planes were being employed with less élan than in the earlier years of the war, there were still ample opportunities for the individualist to kill or be killed.

Russia finally signed the treaty of Brest-Litovsk on March 3, 1918, officially freeing the German divisions on that front for duty in the west. Curiously, both Manfred and Lothar von Richthofen accompanied the German delegation to Brest-Litovsk, although the brothers, bored with the political

Von Richthofen saluting the Kaiser during an inspection of the Flying Circus
JARRETT COLLECTION

Ernst Udet, second only to Richthofen on Germany's aces list. Udet had the distinction of destroying an English tank from the air, a rare accomplishment. He attacked the tank until it turned over. An important figure in the rise of the German Luftwaffe prior to the Second World War, Udet committed suicide when he fell out of grace during the war with his chief, Goering
JARRETT COLLECTION

Douglas Campbell, of the 94th Aero Squadron ("Hat in Ring"), one of the first American-trained pilots to score an aerial victory. The date was April 14, 1918— less than a month after Campbell began operational flights     U. S. AIR FORCE

wrangling, left before the signing to do some hunting before returning to the front. They were anxious to return, for the Germans were excitedly discussing their planned March offensive in the west. It was the plan of Gen. Erich von Ludendorff to smash the British sector in the Somme valley on a fifty-mile front between Arras and Noyon. Ludendorff had seventy divisions to hurl upon the twenty-six of the British.

At 4:45 A.M., March 21, 1918, almost six thousand German guns began firing in the most concentrated artillery bombardment up to that time, to open the Great Battle—and the first of five German offensives that year, desperate and futile attempts to win the war. The opening guns of the March offensive pulverized the earth for five hours, deafening and stunning those who were not killed. Then the German advance began, a seemingly unstoppable wave of field gray. The advance did not come to a halt until April 5.

The men of the Richthofen Circus were disappointed. *Der Tag* had finally come and fog had interfered with their activities. But in the following days, Jagdeschwader No. 1 found plenty of action fighting the Allied planes that had come out to strafe the German troops moving in against the British Fifth and Third Armies. On March 25, the Red Baron shot down a Camel, bring-

Orderlies assist Richthofen in preparing for flight. Such protective clothing and the fur boots were rarely used in the early months of the air war

JARRETT COLLECTION

Von Richthofen and his dog, Moritz          JARRETT COLLECTION

Oberst. Hermann Thomsen, von Richthofen and Commander of the Air Service, General W. von Hoeppner. Both Thomsen and von Hoeppner had proved willing to listen to the early advice of Boelcke, which not only produced an outstanding air force but also a von Richthofen          JARRETT COLLECTION

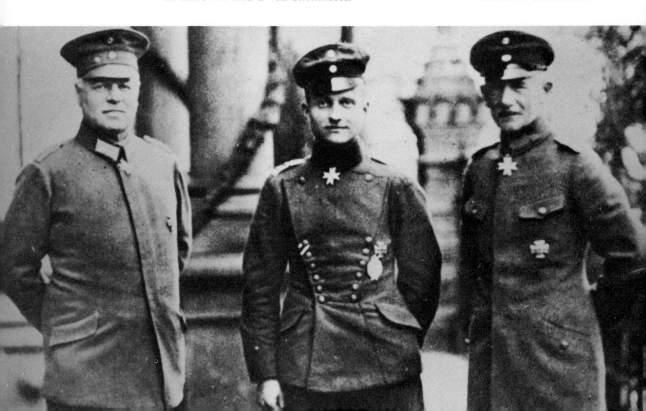

ing his score up to 68. The next day J.G. 1 was joined by another brilliant ace, Ernst Udet, who had commanded Jasta 37. Udet's own score of nineteen victories was an important factor in Richthofen's decision to invite the happy-go-lucky young pilot to join the famed Circus.

As a fledgling pilot Udet had found it difficult to curb his own enthusiasms and self-confidence. He once spent a week in the guardhouse for having foolishly crashed a plane. His skill as a pilot in time revealed him as an outstanding air fighter although his earliest fights might have seemed to deny this. On his first time out he met a French Caudron and could not bring himself to attack it. He finally forced himself to attack a Farman bomber in March 1916—motivated by the thought that the French plane would bomb his fellow countrymen—and brought it down. It was the first of 62 Allied aircraft that would be shot down by Udet. He would live through the war in fact, be second only to von Richthofen on the aces listing and live to revive the German Luftwaffe for World War II. (He did not survive that war, however. Udet committed suicide under the pressures of the Nazis, particularly his chief, Goering.)

Possibly the most dramatic air battle fought by Udet occurred in June 1917 when he met Guynemer in *Vieux Charles*. The German was flying an Albatros D-Va, a good aircraft but not structurally as strong as the French Spad. For almost ten minutes the two planes maneuvered around trying to place a telling burst into an enemy plane (or pilot), and it appeared that while both were fine pilots, the better plane might decide the battle.

Then Udet's guns jammed; as he attempted to clear them, Guynemer moved in for the kill and then apparently saw the German pilot desperately hammering away at the breeches of the guns. But Guynemer did not fire. "Then it happened," Udet reported later. "I looked up to see what he would do with me now. I was at his mercy. I could hardly believe my eyes. He put out one hand, waved to me and dove away to the west, letting me fly home unhurt."

On his first patrol with the Richthofen, flying the Fokker Triplane for the first time, Udet shot down an English R. E. 8 and soon was placed in command of Jasta 11. When the excellent Fokker D-VII was introduced in the spring of 1918, Udet found it a better plane than the triplane, which evidenced a fatal tendency to crumple up in the air under battle stress. Udet's Fokker D-VII was gaily decorated with alternating red and white diagonal stripes on the top of the upper wing; on his elevators he had had painted the words *"Du Doch Nicht!"* ("No, not you!"). On the side of the fuselage the word "Lo!" in oversized letters appeared, a tribute to Udet's fiancée, Lo Zink. Besides ending the war as Germany's Number Two ace, Udet also made an additional mark on aviation history by being one of the few airmen of the war whose life was saved by using a parachute.

By early April the impetus of the German offensive had subsided. On the first of that month the British Royal Air Force was formed, by combining the R. F. C. and the R. N. A. S. The giant step toward full recognition of the air force as an independent service was taken.

179

Captain Roy Brown, standing beside his Sopwith Camel. Brown's final victory total came to twelve, one of which was believed to be Germany's Red Knight. Others, however, were to try to claim the honor of killing Richthofen, long after the First World War was over          ROYAL CANADIAN AIR FORCE

British soldiers inspecting the wreckage of Richthofen's triplane. Souvenir hunters carried away much of the aircraft, although it landed practically undamaged
JARRETT COLLECTION

Examining the Spandau machine guns of Richthofen's Fokker
JARRETT COLLECTION

On April 14, the first American air patrol was finally flown; Capt. David McKelvey Peterson led Lts. Reed Chambers and Edward Rickenbacker over the lines. On standby duty were Lts. Douglas Campbell and Alan Winslow, also of the 94th Aero Squadron. Although the patrol itself was uneventful, the disappointed Campbell and Winslow were the first to score for the 94th. When two German planes materialized out of the mist near the airfield at Toul, the two eager young Americans leaped into their Nieuports and within minutes sent both intruders down in flames. Winslow's victim, a Pfalz D-III, struck first, so he was given the honor of scoring the first victory for the American Air Service. (This was to differentiate between the prior victories by members of the Lafayette Escadrille and other Americans who served in British or French air units.)

For the German Air Service, April was, indeed, "the cruelest month." On the twenty-first, Manfred von Richthofen took off leading five other J.G. 1 pilots. Part of the morning, before the mist cleared away, was spent in horse-play, unusual for the *Rittmeister* (he had kicked the support of a cot upon which one of his pilots was napping; when another came to take the place of the upended pilot, Richthofen repeated the joke). He was in a good mood—his official score stood at eighty, the highest of any airman of the war.

Over the lines, after having been joined also by a flight from Jasta 5, the German planes dived upon two British R. E. 8s of No. 3 Squadron out on a photographic mission. In the ensuing melee, the German planes had moved over the British lines where they came under antiaircraft fire.

A patrol of Camels from No. 209 Squadron led by Canadian Capt. Arthur Royal Brown, attracted by the puffs of A. A. fire, turned to attack the German formation. The two formations came together in a confused dogfight, the results of which have not been resolved to this day.

As patrol leader, Brown felt himself responsible for the lives of his men and in the confusion of falling Triplanes and Camels, he saw that his friend, Lt. W. R. May, was in trouble; a red triplane had attached itself to May's tail. Brown was doubly concerned because it was May's first offensive patrol and inexperience could be fatal.

May had been instructed to stay out of the fighting but he had not been able to let the opportunity pass by and was about to pay for his eagerness if something was not done soon. "Through lack of experience," May said after the battle, "I held one of my guns open too long; it jammed and then the other. I could not clear them so I spun out of the mess and headed west by sun for home. After I leveled out, I looked around, but nobody was following. Feeling pretty good at having extricated myself, the next thing I knew, I was being fired at from behind! All I could do was to try to dodge my attacker, which was a red triplane. Had I known it was Richthofen—I should probably have passed out on the spot!"

Brown had no idea who the German pilot was, but he did know his friend, and charge, was in serious trouble. He dived after the two planes, which had now come very close to the floor of the Somme valley. Even though he was at a great distance from the German plane, Brown fired at the triplane. All three aircraft were close to the ground, the two in front passing over the gun positions of the 53rd Battery, Australian Field Artillery, 5th Australian Division. Ground fire was aimed at the red triplane.

Brown fired another long burst, which, according to Brown's combat report, went "into him and he went down vertical and was observed to crash by Lieut. [F.J.W.] Mellersh and Lieut. May."

The Canadian pilot, having attended to his friend's predicament, turned to two other triplanes but "did not get them." He did not see the red triplane land.

The plane was seen to move erratically for a moment; then it sideslipped, circled and glided down to the ground. In landing, the undercarriage was broken but the triplane was practically intact. It rested in the open ground in full view of both the Germans and British. As the British soldiers watched, they saw that the pilot made no attempt to leave the plane.

They could read the numbers on the side of the Fokker: 425/17, which meant nothing to them. But when the occupant was pulled out of the cockpit and his identification papers examined, all were astonished to learn that he was Richthofen. He had been killed by a single bullet through the chest.

So celebrated was Richthofen on both sides of the line that the controversy over who deserved the credit for shooting him down began. Chief among a number of claimants was Robert Buie, an Australian gunner then serving with the 53rd Battery, who had, like so many other ground men, fired at the red triplane as it flew over the Somme. Other men also claimed to have shot down the great German airman, but only Brown and Buie seem to have the edge on all contenders for the honors. Proponents of each, after meticulous research (some of it gleaned from memories dimmed and romanticized with age), bring forth cogent arguments favoring their special hero. Interservice rivalry (ground forces vs. the air) plays no little part in the controversy.

It seemed terribly important at the time that proper credit be given to the man who killed the great Red Baron, and the controversy began. One doctor, G. C. Graham, who was serving with the 5th Canadian Field Ambulance, examined Richthofen immediately after the red triplane came down. It was the doctor's opinion that if Richthofen had been hit from the ground he would have had to have been flying upside down and toward his own lines. Who the killer of Manfred von Richthofen was will never actually be known, but April 21, 1918 may well go down in history as the day the war stood still.

The British gave Richthofen a funeral, complete with full military honors, on April 22. It was an impressive ceremony, worthy of a respected enemy, complete with a bearer party of six captains (peers of Richthofen's), cortege and firing squad.

The Germans, meanwhile, were in suspense. A front-line observation post had reported: "Red triplane landed on hill near Corbie. Landed all right. Passenger has not left plane." German artillery did not fire on the plane so that its passenger, who seemed capable of landing his plane, might be removed and given medical attention. By evening it was known who the passenger was; his fate was not known until a British pilot flew over Richthofen's home base, at Cappy, and dropped this message:

```
    To,-
            The German Flying Corps.

Rittmeister Baron  MANFRIED  von  RICHTOFEN

was    killed    in    aerial  combat

on    April    21st.    1918.

He   was    buried    with    full

military    honours.
```

Note showing von Richthofen's flower-covered grave, dropped by British airmen behind the German lines

James Thomas Byford McCudden, fourth-ranking British ace and teacher of Edward "Mick" Mannock. McCudden was assigned to command No. 60 Squadron in 1918 and died, aged 22, during his flight to take command of the unit

Edward Mannock, British ace of aces. That he was such was not even known during the war. Mannock, who was in Turkey when the war began, was interned as an enemy alien and then repatriated because of poor health and defective eyesight; he was also considered overage for military service (twenty-seven). But a ferocious hatred for the enemy impelled Mannock not only to enlist but also somehow to get into the air force. Despite the bad eye he was a crack shot; an excellent instructor besides and concerned with the well-being of his student pilots, Mannock showed another side of his character in his love for killing Germans

This typical expression of honest opinion was not shared by every member of the R. A. F. At least one very important member refused to toast the memory of "a chivalrous foe," and in fact left the mess, muttering, "I hope he roasted all the way down." This was hardly the majority view of knightly attitudes but it was the realistic opinion of Edward Mannock, who had enlisted to kill Germans.

The son of a British soldier who had deserted his family while Mannock was still a boy, he was not of the gentlemanly class, nor did he believe in fighting a gentlemanly war. After bluffing his way into the air service (despite the fact that he only had one good eye), Mannock earned himself a reputation for cowardice because of his conservative fighting style. He was not re-

Wilhelm Reinhard, who followed von Richthofen as commander of J.G. 1, according to the latter's wish (left in the form of a handwritten note). Renamed the Richthofen Geschwader, it was led by Reinhard until his death in an accident in which his aircraft shed its wings at 3,000 feet. In this photo Reinhard stands beside his Fokker triplane, which suffered a typical accident: the fabric of the upper wing peeled off                              JARRETT COLLECTION

garded as a very good pilot either—at first. But in time Mannock's cautious, almost scientific handling of aircraft and guns made him an outstanding air leader. He also was the British ace of aces of the war with a score of 73 enemy aircraft shot down. Mannock was an exponent of the new tactical doctrine of formation flying and careful marksmanship. He was a meticulous planner and took excellent care of his flight members, often setting up a victory and then letting the new pilot finish off the enemy plane.

Mannock made no secret of enjoying watching a German descend in flames; he hated war but he burned with an intense hatred for "the Hun." That he ever developed into a skilled air fighter might be attributed to the fact that he had taken training from James McCudden (No. 4 British ace with 57 victories). Like Mannock, McCudden was a superb patrol leader and not of the individualistic school of aerial fighting. In July 1918 McCudden, after a rather long stay in England, was assigned to command No. 60 Squadron. On his way to take over his new command Major McCudden, in his S. E. 5A, experienced engine failure and crashed to his death on a takeoff.

McCudden's death greatly affected Mannock, who swore the Hun would pay for the death of his friend (the illogic seemed immaterial at the time) and led his patrols with even greater determination than he had before. But later in that same month Mannock, too, "went west."

Mannock was in command of No. 85 Squadron and had taken out a new

185

Although he was forced to drop out of McGill University (Montreal) because of poor health in 1914, Donald R. MacLaren managed, in 1917, to enlist in the Royal Flying Corps. Later in the year he was posted to No. 46 Squadron in France to fly the Sopwith Camel. A crack shot—MacLaren had learned to shoot as a boy in Canada—he soon proved himself to be a deadly air fighter. On a single day in March 1918, MacLaren in company with seven other men of No. 46 Squadron bombed out a German long-range gun. He scored two direct hits upon the gun, which was put out of action. Then, en route to his base, MacLaren attacked a German two-seater and shot it down in flames, after which he almost collided with a German balloon obscured in a cloud, turned and shot that down. Feeling perhaps there was more action to be experienced in the vicinity, MacLaren skirted around the clouds until he spotted another German two-seater, which he also shot down. The score for the day stood at: one big gun, one balloon and two observation planes. By war's end, MacLaren commanded No. 46 Squadron; he had shot down 54 enemy aircraft (including in this score 6 balloons) and was sixth on the British aces list ROYAL CANADIAN AIR FORCE

pilot, Lt. D. C. Inglis, on an offensive patrol. They spotted an enemy two-seater and sent it down in flames, but for some reason (perhaps it was his Hun-hatred), Mannock led Inglis down after the two-seater and put more shots into it even after it had hit the ground. Satisfied that the pilot and observer were dead, Mannock led Inglis back toward their lines.

They were now only about 200 feet over the German trenches and under heavy ground fire. Suddenly Inglis saw his leader's S. E. 5 dip—"a small flame and some smoke flicking out from the right side of the plane"—then it spun into the ground and burst into flames. Forgetting his own peril on seeing the great Mannock fall, Inglis circled over the burning S. E. 5 until his plane was hit in the engine and he had to glide toward the English trenches, there crashing. Rescued by Welsh infantrymen, Inglis returned to tell of Mannock's end. Neither Mannock's plane nor his body was ever found by the British, although the Germans had reported burying the great patrol leader. He had roasted all the way down.

Mannock had taken over No. 85 Squadron from William Avery Bishop, the Canadian-born airman. One of the last of the individualists, his name ap-

186

William Avery Bishop in the cockpit of his Nieuport. The second-ranking British ace, Bishop served in both world wars. He was one of the last of the individualists besides being a fine instructor and pilot                    ROYAL CANADIAN AIR FORCE

peared on the British aces list in the number two position, just following Mannock's. Bishop had been retired from the combat lists to preserve his particular aerial genius for training other fighter pilots and for guidence in the organization of a Canadian Air Force. Bishop, a one-time cavalryman, flew the Nieuport during the early phase of his air career. His first victory occurred on March 25, 1917, and much of his operational flying was done during the hazardous days of "Bloody April." Bishop exhibited both a fine skill and a fighting spirit of unusual impact. He once attacked a German airdrome alone early in the morning of June 2, 1917, and shot down three Albatros scouts which were taking off to intercept him. For this daring exploit, and for bringing home his damaged Nieuport 17, Bishop was awarded the Victoria Cross. His importance as an instructor and leader was responsible for Bishop's being

187

The Nieuport 28, last of the wartime line of French fighters. At first widely used by American pilots, its tendency to lose fabric off the top wing made it unpopular. It was, however, a clean design and faster than earlier Nieuports, capable of a top speed of 140-mph                                                    U. S. AIR FORCE

away from the front a great deal, although he did return after one of his absences, to command No. 85 Squadron. In a period of less than two weeks he shot down twenty-five enemy planes, twelve of them in his last three days before being transferred away from the front.

Serving under Bishop in No. 85 Squadron were several Americans, among them Lawrence Calahan of Chicago, John McGavock Grider of Memphis, and Elliot White Springs of Lancaster, South Carolina. The latter, who probably was the prototype for every hell-raising, wenching and drinking airman portrayed in the postwar aviation films, was indeed a hell raiser, drinker and wencher. He was also an excellent flier, a writer, and shared fifth place on the American ace list (all with 12 victories) with Capt. Field E. Kindley and Lt. David E. Putnam. Springs managed to live through the war and edited Grider's diary (no doubt adding much material of his own), after Grider was shot down and disappeared without a trace. Published as *War Birds—Diary of an Unknown Aviator,* the book is one of the classics of World War I.

Springs, Grider and Calahan ("Cal" in the book) were among a group of 150 aviators, many of them Princetonians, who had set out aboard the R.M.S. *Carmania* in September 1917 for Italy. Aboard the same ship was Capt. Fiorello La Guardia, who eventually ended up in Italy in an American bombardment group. Through some typical confusion, Springs and his impatient Princetonians disembarked in England and were shipped off to Oxford for a

Elliot White Springs, in U. S. uniform and wearing the wings of the U. S. Air Service. Springs flew the S.E. 5 with the British No. 85 Squadron and Sopwith Camels with the American 148th Aero Squadron. Of wealthy Southern parentage, Springs was an ace with 12 victories to his credit. After the war he returned to his native South Carolina to run the family cotton mills—after a fling at a writing career                                        U. S. SIGNAL CORPS: NATIONAL ARCHIVES

A squadron lineup of S.E. 5As in France; the unit is No. 85 Squadron, commanded by William Bishop, in which many American pilots served, among them the dashing Elliot White Springs                                        JARRETT COLLECTION

repeat of the ground schooling they had already received at Princeton. Many would go on to flight school and would begin their combat service with British units.

The so-called "Three Musketeers"—Springs, Calahan and Grider—went to Bishop's No. 85 Squadron; George A. Vaughn of Brooklyn flew S. E. 5As with No. 84 Squadron, R. F. C. and Lt. Walter Chalaire, ex-reporter of the New York *Herald,* was assigned to No. 2 Squadron, R. N. A. S., in which he flew the D. H. 4—the British machine powered by the Rolls-Royce engine

America's third-ranking ace, George A. Vaughn, Jr., who served with the British No. 84 Squadron and with the American 17th Aero Squadron. While with the R.A.F., Vaughn shot down 7 of his officially credited enemy aircraft. He received the Distinguished Flying Cross from the British for a patrol which Vaughn reported thus: "While on an offensive patrol with 'B' Flight, my Flight Commander dived on an enemy captive balloon, just south of the Somme. I broke away from the formation, and dived on a second balloon on the opposite bank of the river. I opened fire with my Vickers at fairly long range, and the observer jumped out in his parachute. At about 100 yards, I fired around 50 rounds of flat-nosed Buckingham from my Lewis, and was then so close that I had to zoom away. As I turned to get in another burst of Buckingham, the balloon burst into flame"

GEORGE A. VAUGHN, JR.

and not the American Liberty. These men regarded themselves as fortunate because they were able to serve with the British forces, although later, like so many other Americans who had trained with the British and French, they transferred to American units. Chalaire served his entire combat career with the British, however, and finished his tour with No. 202 Squadron, R. A. F. when the R. F. C. and R. N. A. S. were amalgamated into the Royal Air Force.

George Vaughn was assigned to the 17th Aero Squadron; Springs, Grider and Calahan served the American 148th Aero Squadron (Grider died on June 18, 1918). Both these squadrons, although American, were under British operational control and, it might be noted, received a good deal less newspaper coverage than was lavished on the units in the American-controlled sectors.

Many Americans who served, particularly with the British, harbored little love for American air officers, or worse, the West Pointers who believed in a picture-book war fought according to the manuals. Typical of the latter was a major who dropped in from Paris to see the American cadets at Oxford. As reported by Grider/Springs in *War Birds,* he "certainly did despise us in public with a loud voice." One of the major's most serious objections was to

Gen. Benjamin D. Foulois, Chief of the American Air Service, and Gen. John J. Pershing, Commander of the American Expeditionary Forces in Europe. This photo was taken when Pershing visited the Issoudon Air Field at which American pilots were trained for combat during the First World War        U. S. AIR FORCE

the uniform the Americans wore: it wasn't smart enough. He ordered all the men to have proper uniforms tailored (at their own expense) so that they would look like real soldiers. The wealthy Springs helped the men under him (he was a sergeant then) to acquire this necessity—else how could the war continue?—having armed himself with a generous letter of credit. "I hope some day to meet him again," wrote the *War Bird,* giving voice to the wish of at least 99 percent of all who ever served in an army. "He's one man that ought to have his face shoved down his throat."

Getting the American effort under way was a complex operation, and all did not go well. There was much talk and little action. Industrialists were promising great armadas of aircraft which would smash the hated foe, but such armadas were not forthcoming. American aviation development had not progressed much beyond the Wright brothers' *Flyer,* and although great ad-

191

American planes over France—the Curtiss JN-4 "Jenny." The Jenny was used widely as a trainer but never as a combat aircraft. It was designed as a trainer, however, and proved to be a fine, sturdy ship and remained in use long after the war (until 1927 by the U. S. Air Corps), especially by barnstorming stunt pilots

Gen. Benjamin D. Foulois standing before the DeHavilland 4, the D.H. 4, the American-built plane that was to become known as the "Flaming Coffin." An excellent day bomber and reconnaissance aircraft, the D.H. 4, despite the reputation for bursting into flame for no reason, developed into one of the outstanding aircraft of the war. The British version was powered by the Rolls-Royce engine and the American by the mass-produced Liberty

David E. Putnam (left), ex-Lafayette Escadrille member, with his commanding officer, Capt. D. L. Hill of the 139th Aero Squadron. A descendant of the Revolutionary War Gen. Israel Putnam, young Putnam served with the Lafayette Escadrille for several months. He experienced his most famous battle when attacked by 10 German Albatros fighters and shot 5 of them down single-handed. His final official score stood at 12, but it is believed it was actually closer to 30. Putnam was killed in combat in September 1918

U. S. SIGNAL CORPS: NATIONAL ARCHIVES

vances had been made by the warring powers during 1914-1917, such advances, naturally enough, were kept highly secret. When the United States went to war, it had no warplane worthy of the name. American airmen fought in French and British planes.

General Pershing quickly sensed that something was wrong with the American aviation branch and placed his friend Mason M. Patrick in charge, with a note informing him:

> In all this Army, there is but one thing which is causing me anxiety, and that is the Air Service. In it are a lot of good men, but they are running around in circles. Someone has got to make them go straight. I want you to do it.

The problem confronting Patrick, who had never been up in an airplane, was stated succinctly by Col. H. A. Toulmin who wrote:

> The Air Service stood, in May 1918, practically a complete failure. A great bulk of nearly 30,000 Air Service men was scattered in isolated units, planeless and purposeless, too conscious perhaps of their own dig-

nity and not enough of their sacred opportunities and obligations. Briefly, the Air Service had no organization.

Brig. Gen. Benjamin D. Foulois, who had been Chief of Air Service, A.E.F., was reassigned to Chief of Air Service, First Army, in the resultant shakeup. Foulois' staff had been torn by internal dissensions, personal jealousies and the classic friction between air and ground officers. Patrick brought order to the chaos; as the confusion and anger cleared away there emerged an airman of imagination and ability who would command the American air forces in Europe: Brig. Gen. William Mitchell.

Mitchell, one of the most controversial and outspoken individuals in American military history, was an advocate of the use of strategic air power, a point of view he shared with Britain's Hugh Trenchard.

The United States was not militarily prepared for war, especially not for the war in the air. Not one American military plane, for example, saw action at the front. The only useful American-designed plane was the Curtiss JN-4, the famed "Jenny," which was an excellent training ship but whose lack of maneuverability canceled out its combat worthiness. Under contract, American manufacturers turned out the English-designed DeHaviland D.H. 4s, which were powered by the American-designed Liberty engine. Only a few of these arrived at the front to see action.

The growing pains of an awakening giant, resulting in inefficiency (which looked especially bad after the vaunting promises of the Aircraft Production Board for "regiments and brigades of winged cavalry mounted on gas-driven flying horses" which would "sweep the Germans from the sky"), impaired the air effort of the United States. But if the industrial contribution fell below the hoped-for "clouds of planes" and if internal squabbling compounded the confusion, the American fliers proved themselves worthy of the company of great fighting airmen they had come to join.

With America's entry into the war the fate of the Lafayette Escadrille became a problem. This was readily solved by absorbing the unit out of the French Air Service into the American Air Service as the 103rd Aero Squadron of the Third Pursuit Group on February 18, 1918. The internal situation being as it was, it was not until six months later that the 103rd Aero Squadron moved into the American sector. One of the reasons for delay was that the American airmen, although supplied with French aircraft, often found the planes to be obsolete and without guns.

Of the original seven members—Chapman, McConnell, Prince, Rockwell, Cowdin, Hall and Thaw—only the last three were still alive when the Escadrille was taken into the U. S. Air Service. Some of the later squadron personnel chose to remain with the French, among them Edwin C. Parsons and Didier Masson; some could not pass the physical examinations and were declared unfit to do that which they had been doing for the past year or two. William Thaw, one of the original seven, was commissioned a major in the U. S. Army and placed in command of the 103rd Aero Squadron. An excel-

Raoul Lufbery seated in his gift from the manufacturer, the Hispano-Suiza Company, which also made aircraft engines. Lufbery was among the many members of the Lafayette Escadrille who transferred to the American Air Service in 1918

lent administrator, Thaw became commander of the Third Pursuit Group, comprised of the 28th, 93rd, 103rd and 213th Aero Squadrons.

Among those who transferred from the Lafayette Escadrille into the U. S. Air Service was the Escadrille's ace of aces, Raoul Lufbery. Like Thaw, Lufbery was commissioned a major, but unlike Thaw the Americans could not find the right spot for him. Lufbery, a man of action, was assigned to a desk at Issoudon in a purely administrative post. "The crass stupidity of certain American brass hats failed to recognize his value as a fine fighter," Edwin C. Parsons was to comment on the situation. "They gave him the rank of major in American aviation and equipped him with a pretty uniform and a pair of spurs; then they let him eat his heart out, sitting for months at a desk doing nothing."

This was an exaggeration, for Lufbery spent about a month at Issoudon. In addition, he spent much time in hospitals with attacks of rheumatism. The American attitude was also predicated by a concern with the value of an experienced fighter who could teach the young fliers all he had learned in the

195

Members of the 94th Aero Squadron in France, most of them pupils of Raoul Lufbery. They are Joseph Eastman, James Meissner, Edward Rickenbacker, Reed Chambers and Thorne Taylor      U. S. SIGNAL CORPS: NATIONAL ARCHIVES

years he had spent fighting. Lufbery's official score by this time had reached seventeen, although unofficially he had undoubtedly accounted for twice that number.

Lufbery was finally posted to the 95th Aero Squadron and then was sent to the 94th, as commanding officer for a while, in April 1918. The 94th Aero Squadron was the first American unit to get into action—once its planes had been fitted with guns. Lufbery proved to be a fine instructor and among his students were James Meissner, Reed Chambers, Douglas Campbell and Edward V. Rickenbacker.

Rickenbacker, a former racing driver who had served for a time as General Pershing's staff driver, was comparatively older than the average airman. He was twenty-seven when he began flying (a pilot's age was generally closer to twenty), a careful tactician who analyzed the glamorous air war in a phrase by saying, "I can see that aerial warfare is actually scientific murder."

Rickenbacker brought mature thinking, technical knowledge and precise technique to air fighting and in his first month in combat he had become an ace. Despite the fact that he was hospitalized for fifteen weeks with a serious ear infection, Rickenbacker returned to the 94th Squadron (which he eventually commanded) to become America's highest scoring airman. He was awarded the Medal of Honor for attacking a Fokker formation of five planes, shooting one down in flames, and then turning to two Halberstadts and succeeded in shooting one of those down also. Rickenbacker's final score was twenty-two aircraft and four balloons.

Balloons were never a favorite target, but they were always a serious threat to the ground forces. Captive balloons could observe movement and alert their forces, or they could direct field artillery fire; it was difficult for the infantry to make a move while a "sausage" floated above the lines. Balloons were therefore valuable and were heavily protected. To attack them was considered near, or even certain, suicide.

One of the units in the First Pursuit Group along with the 94th was the 27th Aero Squadron, whose most notorious member was an unpopular young madman who specialized in "balloon busting." His name was Frank Luke, Jr., of Phoenix, Arizona, and he displayed the kind of fighting spirit and disdain for discipline that had, by 1918, gone out of style. Luke was a brooding loner who found formation flying a bore and a handicap. He frequently left patrols to go hunting on his own, later returning to his base claiming to have shot down an enemy plane. He was called a liar and generally ostracized by his squadron mates, who had had to complete their patrol minus the two guns Luke might have contributed to their defense in an attack.

The attitude of his fellow fliers only caused Luke to keep more to himself. Finally on September 12, 1918, Luke destroyed his first German balloon; whereupon the Arizonan landed at a nearby American balloon position to get official confirmation from two witnesses—he was taking no chances. But when he attempted to take off, he found that in the attack upon the balloon his Spad had been so badly shot up that it could not leave the ground. Luke had his first officially confirmed victory—and seventeen days to live.

Another outcast in the 27th Aero Squadron was Joseph Fritz Wehner, who, because of his German descent (although he had been born in Boston), had been harassed all through his military career. He had served as a volunteer in German prison camps before the United States' entry into the war and the suspicion was that he harbored German sympathies. It was after Luke had shot down his first balloon that he and Wehner formed an aerial partnership. As the squadron's two pariahs, they found a common meeting ground; they were also concerned with fighting the war. Wehner shot down seven enemy aircraft before he himself was killed during an attack on a balloon. It happened when Wehner had attacked six Fokkers which had come after Luke, unaware of the German planes. Wehner was shot down and Luke, who did

Captain Edward V. Rickenbacker, American "Ace of Aces"

not see the fight, returned to his field and announced that he had shot down two balloons and three German planes in ten minutes.

The death of Wehner upset Luke, who was sent to Paris on leave but returned before the leave was up. He then formed another team with Lt. Ivan Roberts, who was also shot down. Luke was now on his own; he came and went as he wished and was reported as AWOL, reprimanded and threatened. But this meant nothing to Luke. In desperation, Luke's commanding officer grounded him until he could learn to conform to the regulations of the air service. In answer to that, Luke merely took off in his Spad and headed for the front. The day was September 29, 1918; had he returned from that flight, Luke would have been court-martialed. Instead, he did not return and was awarded the Medal of Honor.

As he flew over the front Luke dropped a note advising an American balloon company to WATCH THREE HUN BALLOONS ON MEUSE. Within minutes

Frank Luke, Jr., second-ranking American ace, who made his name as a "balloon buster." The diffident—and difficult—Luke was looked upon by his squadron mates as a braggart and headstrong grandstander. Luke was actually a withdrawn type who found it difficult to make friends or to conform to military discipline. He was a crack shot and a skilled pilot, though foolishly headlong as a tactician

the three *drachen* were flaming and falling to the ground. Luke was attacked by a swarm of Fokkers. Luke had either been wounded while attacking the balloons or during the assault by the German fighters, for he landed his Spad near the village of Murvaux, behind the German lines. According to witnesses, he strafed German troops in the streets of Marvaux, killing six men. Luke died beside his Spad in a battle with some of these same troops. With his score of twenty-one victories, Frank Luke was the second-highest-scoring American ace. He was undoubtedly the last of the lone eagles, the individua-

199

America's ace of aces, Edward Rickenbacker. As good an administrator as he was
a pilot, Rickenbacker was also commanding officer of the 94th Aero Squadron.
Although he transferred to the Air Service after a short military career as
Pershing's official driver and lost much time from combat with a serious ear
infection, Rickenbacker evolved such efficient fighting tactics that he scored
twenty-six victories before the war ended                    U. S. AIR FORCE

lists who regarded the war as a private sport and who, for all their courage
and skill, wasted their lives in showmanship.

Luke, for all the attention he has received, was not the war's only balloon
buster. The leading balloon ace of the war, in fact, was France's Michel Coiffard, who shot down twenty-eight *drachen*. Willy Coppens, Belgian ace of
aces, burned twenty-six German gasbags. On one of these missions he experienced one of the war's unique adventures. On May 15, 1918, he attacked a
balloon while flying his favorite plane, the Hanriot D-I. Firing at almost
point-blank range without apparent effect, Coppens flew in closer and fired

A German Hannover CL-III, a two-seater fighter aircraft also employed in strafing trenches. Unusual feature was the biplane tail. This Hannover was brought down practically intact by Rickenbacker and Reed Chambers on October 2, 1918. Rickenbacker and Chambers frequently flew as a team, which is how they dealt with the Hannover. Rickenbacker attacked first and was himself attacked by five Fokkers hidden in a cloud. The observer was killed but the pilot was unhurt. Chambers then came in, wounded the pilot, and forced him down; the plane was so new, Chambers reported, "you could still smell the varnish"

U. S. SIGNAL CORPS: NATIONAL ARCHIVES

again. Suddenly the balloon rose upward, colliding with the little Hanriot. The wheels sank into the gas bag and the plane began nosing over. Quickly Coppens cut off his engine and the balloon, with the plane astride, began settling to the ground. As it tipped further, the Hanriot slipped off and dived. When it reached flying speed, Coppens flipped on the engine and pulled out in time to see the now burning *drachen* continue its fall.

One of Germany's most famous balloon specialists was Heinrich Gontermann, who downed eighteen balloons and twenty-one aircraft before he him-

Reed Chambers, American ace of the 94th Aero Squadron, later commanding officer of the First Pursuit Group. Chambers shot down five planes and a balloon. When he was assigned to attack the balloon on what was considered a suicide mission, Chambers flew with the feeling he had "a mouthful of cotton all the way across the lines." Balloons were always unpopular targets    REED CHAMBERS

self was killed. Gontermann was not shot down in combat, however; he died after the top wing of his Fokker Triplane folded up in the air.

In one of the neglected war theaters—Macedonia—twenty-year-old Rudolph von Eschwege fought a gallant war against the English. Though outnumbered, Eschwege proved a most formidable enemy, accounting for nineteen aircraft, most of them balloons of the British balloon company near his base at Drama. Eschwege's intrepidity forced the British to devise a fiendish —and not very sportsmanlike—method of dealing with him. Instead of an observer, a dummy was sent up in the basket of a balloon along with 500 pounds of high explosive. When Eschwege's Albatros moved in close to the balloon, the explosive was detonated from the ground. Balloon, Albatros and Eschwege were blown to bits.

Historians and writers raise the question about the overemphasis of the deeds of the fighter pilots as compared with the accomplishments of the bombers, observation pilots, and even the fighters in two-seater aircraft. They were the forgotten men of the air services. Once a victory had to be divided by two, shared by pilot and gunner, it lost its impact. Nor did it seem especially interesting to the newspaper reader to learn that a flight of D. H. 4s had dropped bombs upon German troop concentrations. It was a matter of getting there and getting back (and not all got back); if you were attacked, your

202

Willy Coppens (center), Belgium's great aerial ace and a leading balloon buster
IMPERIAL WAR MUSEUM

gunner fought off the enemy while you flew the plane. Two-seater pilots and/or gunners were never called aces, for who could accurately assign credit for victories?

As explained by Lt. Walter R. Lawson, "When a formation of observers get into a dogfight, there is much wild firing by everyone, and it is impossible to tell whose bullet brings down the Fritzie who nose-dives in flames. So it is a custom in all armies to credit officially every pilot and observer in a dog-fight when a Boche takes the count."

The special attention given to the fighter pilots, just as the British had wisely cautioned, had its effect upon the less glorified fighting men, even in the flying services. Just before he "fell gloriously" in flames, Lt. Walter V. Barneby, of the 1st Aero Squadron (Observation Group), had written a let-ter to his mother in Sumner, Washington. "On account of the constant pub-licity of *chasse* work," Barneby wrote, "most people are under the impression that the fast little fighting planes are the only ones to be considered by the elite of the air, while from a purely utilitarian standpoint for the Army they are of small value.

"It is the observation planes that do most of the hard work and get the

203

The 11th Aero Squadron (Bombardment), an American unit which used the
D.H. 4; the squadron insignia is "Jiggs," the popular newspaper cartoon character
U. S. AIR FORCE

least credit for it. They are the eyes of the modern army, and their work is
by far the most important. With the single exception of the low fliers who attack and bomb troops at a few meters' height when a general attack is going
on, observation is the most dangerous of all aviation. The pilot of the observation plane has one or more lives other than his own in his keeping, and his
plane has cost a great deal to produce."

The D. H. 4 was one of the finest of the reconnaissance and bombardment
aircraft, despite its eventual reputation as "The Flaming Coffin." Its major
flaw was the great distance between the cockpits of the pilot and gunner (also
called the "gun-layer"), which made communication during flight difficult;
the placement of the fuel tank between the two cockpits could mean that a
fire in the air placed both crew members in a tough spot. But the D. H. 4 had
the advantages of speed and the ability to operate at a comparatively high
ceiling (22,000 feet with the 375 hp Rolls-Royce engine).

Lt. Walter Chalaire, an American who had come over with Elliot White
Springs and the Princeton group, remained with the British even after the

American units began forming in France. He was posted to No. 2 Squadron, Royal Naval Air Service and was the pilot of a D. H. 4. The airdrome was situated just ten miles from Dunkirk. Chalaire and his gunner-observer Sgt. A. E. Humphrey, were assigned a typical mission in July 1918, a mission which proved to be the last for both.

Two planes were dispatched to photograph some activity in the vicinity of Ostend; the British wished to know if bridges were being thrown over the river as a prelude to a new German push. In order not to arouse suspicion, only two D. H. 4s were dispatched—one to take the photographs and the other, manned by Chalaire and Humphrey, to furnish protection. The mission proceeded without incident until the two planes had begun the return trip. The camera plane and Chalaire's separated, and while he and his observer attempted to find it, they found instead that they were surrounded by Fokkers. There was one flight above them and another just behind and below.

The Germans pounced in for the attack. Chalaire manhandled the heavy D. H. 4 in order to get shots at the attackers and to enable Humphrey to fire also. Two of the Fokkers went down burning, which seems to have discouraged some of the German pilots who left the fight. Even so, no less than eight remained to worry the men in the D. H. The British plane became the focal point for converging fire as fabric peeled away, wires snapped and both men bled from wounds. Chalaire was soon without his forward-firing gun, which jammed (a German bullet had struck a cartridge in the gun belt which exploded and then, misshapen, jammed the breech). In dismay, Chalaire looked back to check on Humphrey and saw that his gunner had disappeared. Certain that his gunner had fallen out of the plane while he had thrown it through its evasive maneuvers, Chalaire—his shoulder now bleeding profusely—realized that he had only one thing to do. He dived for home and succeeded in losing the German fighters in the clouds over Flanders.

Skillfully he brought the tattered D. H. to a landing and was surprised to learn that Humphrey was still in his cockpit, although seriously wounded. Both men required hospitalization—Chalaire with a shoulder wound and Humphrey had been hit seven times. By acting quickly, Chalaire was able to get the needed medical attention for Humphrey, who wrote an appreciative letter from the Royal Infirmary, Dundee, Scotland. Dated August 19, 1918, it is transcribed exactly as Humphrey wrote it:

Lt. Walter Chalaire, ex-reporter on the New York *Herald* who volunteered in 1916 for service in the U. S. aviation section. Like many other Americans, Chalaire was given further training in England after completing initial flying instruction in the U. S. Chalaire became a D.H. 4 pilot with No. 2 Squadron, Royal Naval Air Service (later No. 202 Squadron, R.A.F.), stationed ten miles from Dunkerque. Serving throughout his military career with the British, Chalaire does not recall ever hearing the D.H. 4 referred to as a "Flaming Coffin"

205

Dear Sir:

1st Lt. W. Chalaire

Your letter to hand, I can assure you that I am ever so pleased to have received your letter, and to know that you are making such rapid progress. Are your wounds very serious? Really when you got out of the machine, no one would ever have thought that we had been next to death's door only a few minutes previous, but Sir, there is no praise too great for you, because you are the most wonderful Pilot I have ever been in the air with. The way you threw that "Bus" about, anyone would think it impossible for a machine to stand the strain. It was to your heroic work Sir, that I am here, and not below the ground with a cross above me. At nights especially I have thought of our scramble with the eight Huns, but in spite of the odds against [us], we are still alive to tell the tale. When I saw the petrol pouring out, I dipped my glove into it, and I was going to call your attention, but to my dismay the reins [an endless cable used for sending notes between the cockpits; there was also a speaking tube] had been shot away, so is was impossible to do anything, only to hold on. The gun on the Scarfe Ring packed up after firing about 1¾ trays, so lucky enough, I happened to have my spare gun with me, but unfortunately he [the German] put the life out of my left arm and so compelled me to discontinue firing.

So we have been credited with two Huns, that's the stuff, but when I read your account of how our machine had been riddled with bullets —controls shot away and both petrol tanks peppered, apart from bracing wires, flying wires, struts, etc., it proves that there is no man more worthy of praise and decorations than you. Sir, I am more than thankful for your kindness towards me, and I hope and trust you will be decorated by the U. S. Air Service and also by the British Authorities for your Gallant Bravery. I quite forgot to tell you, my wounds are healing A. 1., the left shoulder and left knee is practically better, and three holes in the right foot, near the toes, are better but the one on the heel and right ankle, also the wound in the right calf are making slow but sure progress.

I was sorry they sent me so far from home, because this is about 360 miles from London altho this is a real good Hospital. I should like to get a transfer nearer home. Well Sir, I must now conclude, thanking you for the letter you wrote to my wife . . . your letter prevented her from taking a bad view of our misfortune, so with the best of luck and a speedy recovery to you Sir,

Believe me,<br>
Yours Obediently,<br>
A. E. HUMPHREY

P.S. Sir: Did Capt. Bowater and his observer receive any injuries? I hope and trust you will write me again.

The next letter from Humphrey proudly had D. F. M. (Distinguished Flying Medal) following his name and "Sergeant" prefixing it. In his letter, the new sergeant asked Lieutenant Chalaire to be assigned again as the lieutenant's

A German balloonist jumping from his basket while under attack; his parachute trails out behind. The chute was not worn on the back but was stored in a compartment above the basket                                                   U. S. WAR DEPT.: NATIONAL ARCHIVES

aerial gunner, once both returned to flying. Neither did, for it took Humphrey a long time to recover and Chalaire's own injuries were serious enough for him to be returned to the United States on the *Mauretania*.

Of the four airmen to receive the Medal of Honor, two were crew members of a D. H. 4 (who like Frank Luke were honored posthumously; Rickenbacker was the other recipient). When the famous Lost Battalion was surrounded in the Argonne, planes of the 50th Aero Squadron were sent out to find it (in truth, the Lost Battalion was neither a battalion or lost, for it actually consisted of several units from the 77th Division—and everyone knew where it was. The Americans, however, were completely surrounded by the Germans and without food or water).

Planes of the 50th Aero Squadron were sent out to drop supplies to the entrapped men. Because the infantrymen did not like to display the white

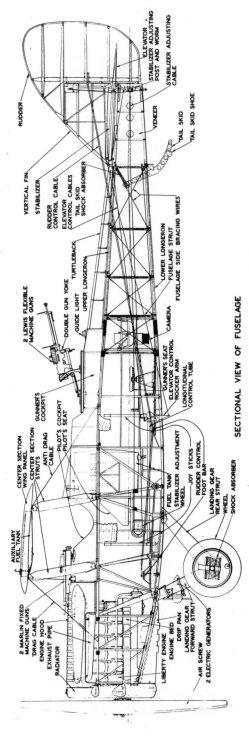

## DEHAVILLAND 4 WITH LIBERTY "12"

Sectional view of the D.H. 4 reproduced from a wartime rigging manual. Positions of the pilot's and observer's seats are indicated as are the location of the weapons of each. A camera was installed just behind the observer's seat for making aerial photographs. The gas tank was positioned in the upper fuselage between the pilot and observer

AIR FORCE MUSEUM

panels used to communicate with the American planes (they said it also gave away their position to the German planes) it was difficult in the dense Argonne to find the exact spot for the supply drop and consequently, none of the food or medical supplies fell into the hands of the Lost Battalion. In his letter to his mother, already cited, Walter V. Barneby touched on the subject of what he called "infantry liaison," a kind of work that did not "happen very often, fortunately for us, as the mortality rate is very high indeed. It happens only when an assault is being undertaken and it calls for the most experienced observers and the most skilled pilots. It is necessary to fly very low, so low that the enemy *chasse* planes make no attempt to bother them, depending on their machine guns on the ground to bring them down."

The Lost Battalion was hidden in a ravine so that when the planes of the 50th Squadron attempted to drop supplies to them, they flew into a valley and the German machine guns on the slopes actually fired down upon the D. H.s. On one of these missions Lts. Erwin R. Bleckley and Harold E. Goettler flew through this valley, pinpointing the positions of the German guns on a map. They came under heavy fire and, both fatally wounded, Goettler, the pilot, lived just long enough to lift the plane out of the ravine and fly it near the French lines; he was dead by the time the French infantry got out to the plane. Bleckley, notes in hand, died shortly after. Other pilots performed with equal heroism: for example, Lts. Maurice Graham and James McCurdy (who was severely wounded), throughout the entire period during which the Americans tried to relieve the trapped men in the pocket. Only Bleckley and Goettler were awarded the Congressional Medal of Honor for "perserverance during a supply dropping mission at Binarville, following which [they] died of wounds."

Men died in the two-seaters, although the newspapers tended to ignore them. It was little comfort to know that you had not died alone.

On the night of 5-6 August, by coincidence a D. H. 4 closed the career of the Chief of the German Naval Airship Division, Peter Strasser, as well as the operations of the Zeppelins. On that night Strasser had ordered out the L-53, L-56, L-63, L-65 and the L-70. The latter was under command of the young Johann von Lossnitzer, who carried as a passenger the Leader of Airships himself: Strasser, leading the first raid on England in four months. It was Lossnitzer's first raid upon England; the L-70 was the latest in the Zeppelin design, the first of the vaunted "height climbers," which could keep out of the range of defending aircraft and artillery fire. It was a massive ship, almost 700 feet long.

The target was not London, but south or middle England. The east coast was quickly alerted and aircraft were dispatched and began climbing for altitude. Leading a flight of three hoping to intercept the airships while they were still over the North Sea was Major Egbert Cadbury with his observer, Capt. Robert Leckie, both of them veterans of the anti-Zeppelin campaign. Cadbury piloted a fine D. H. 4 powered by the Rolls-Royce Eagle engine.

In the faint glow of the evening sky the planes sighted three Zeppelins

Fregattenkapitan Peter Strasser, Chief of the German Naval Airship Service. The champion of the Zeppelin as a weapon of war, Strasser died in the crash of the L-70, shot down over England in the summer of 1918

pointed toward England. Cadbury, at about 16,000 feet, moved in for an attack. His approach was "head on, slightly to port so as to clear any obstructions that might be suspended from airship. My observer trained his gun on the bow of the airship and the fire was seen to concentrate on a spot under the Zeppelin ¾ way aft."

The Pomeroy explosive bullets were "seen to blow a great hole in the fabric and a fire started which quickly ran along the entire length of the Zeppelin. The Zeppelin raised her bows as if in an effort to escape, then plunged seaward a blazing mass." Witnessing the fall of the L-70, Commander Walter Dose (L-65) dropped his bombs harmlessly out at sea (he thought he was bombing antiaircraft gun batteries near King's Lynn, but his bearings were off) and returned to base, although not without some damage from attacking aircraft. The L-53 also dropped its bombs into the sea and headed for Nordholz. The L-56 and L-63 likewise dropped their bombloads into the sea, be-

210

lieving as did the others that they were over England. With the death of Strasser, airship raids against England were ended. He had died a terrible death, for the L-70 burned all the way down to the water and continued to burn even there for nearly an hour. His body and those of the crew, as well as valuable military papers, were recovered. Strasser's funeral pyre, in a sense, was the symbol of the airship's past and future.

Fire was a dreaded occurrence in the air. Airmen probably feared it more than bullets in those days of no self-sealing tanks and few parachutes. It was unnerving to see a man willingly step out of a burning plane, perhaps ten thousand feet in the air, and drop to his death. It was possible at times, by adroit handling of a plane, to fan the flames away from the occupants and with luck to make it to the ground without fatal injury. Lts. Alan McLeod and A. W. Hammond in an Armstrong-Whitworth (popularly called the "Ack-W") were attacked by eight Fokkers, two of which were shot down in the first few minutes of the fight. Then over Albert, France, the Ack-W was hit and burst into flame. The triplanes continued to fire at the British plane. McLeod clambered out onto the wing in order to be able to control the ship without burning, and Hammond returned fire seated on top of the fuselage. A third triplane was shot down.

McLeod sideslipped the burning plane, although both he and Hammond were burned and brought it down in No Man's Land. Hammond had been wounded a number of times, as had McLeod; the crash knocked Hammond unconscious and McLeod managed to pull him out of the burning wreckage. British Tommies finally rescued both fliers from the battleground which was under fire by German artillery. McCleod was given the Victoria Cross for his exploit although he died tragically while recuperating in Canada, a victim of influenza.

Death by burning was a preoccupation of many pilots, among them Raoul Lufbery, who is reported to have said he would rather leap than burn. (Other reports will insist that Lufbery, in his instructing, advised pilots to stay with their planes, even if burning, as long as possible, there always being a chance of making it to the ground. Which of these one chooses depends upon the kind of irony preferred. Most of those who actually knew Lufbery say he said he would jump if afire.)

On a pleasant, sunny Sunday morning (May 10, 1918), an Albatros two-seater appeared over the very airdrome on which the First Pursuit Group was stationed. French antiaircraft guns began sending up puffs of smoke, one of which seemed to knock the Albatros into a spin. But it had only deceived them and pulled up about 200 feet above the ground. One American plane managed to get off the ground, but the inexperienced pilot very quickly expended his ammunition supply in shooting at the German plane from too great a distance.

Lufbery watched with some impatience—his own plane, with its carefully tuned engine and the guns he personally tended, was out of commission. No longer able to contain himself, Lufbery leaped into a Nieuport standing by

Lufbery in American uniform wearing a major's insignia. The plane is a Nieuport, such as Lufbery flew on his last flight    U. S. SIGNAL CORPS: NATIONAL ARCHIVES

and took off. The Albatros had climbed to 2,000 feet by this time and Lufbery swooped in for an attack. He was watched by a great number of his own comrades and ground troops.

He began firing at the Albatros when it came into range but his bullets seemed to take no effect (the German plane, it was later learned, was armor plated.) Then his guns (which were strange to Lufbery) seemed to jam; at least Lufbery stopped firing, circled around behind the Albatros and came in for another attack.

LeRoy Prinz, then an officer with the 94th Aero Squadron (and later a film director), watched the fight from the ground. "Suddenly Raoul Lufbery's Nieuport wobbled and tossed like a stick in a windstorm. A great ball of crimson fanned out from the cockpit." Either the plane had simply caught fire or the German gunner had registered a hit. As his horrified friends watched, Lufbery tried, at first, to sideslip the flames away from his body (the fuel tank of the Nieuport 28 was in the upper portion of the plane just in front of the pilot); his plane was blazing.

The men on the ground saw him leave the cockpit. For a moment Lufbery poised on the wing, then he jumped. He fell, almost hitting a Frenchwoman in her garden in the village of Maron, north of Nancy. His body struck a picket fence and Lufbery died instantly. In his memoirs, Gen. William

212

DeHavilland 9As, of the British Independent Air Force; these planes were the last day bombers to go into service before the end of the war. Issued to No. 110 Squadron, the D.H. 9As flew in defensive formation, as here, and successfully bombed such German cities as Frankfurt, Mannheim and Coblenz

Mitchell described the death of the man who was then the American ace of aces:

Along the fence on both sides was a fringe of flowers. It was on this picket fence that Lufbery had fallen. One of the pickets pierced his left leg and unquestionably greatly broke his fall. He hit the ground and lay on his back, dead.

The shoemaker's daughter rushed to Lufbery's body and opening his flying suit, saw his decorations and recognized him immediately. Lufbery was a great hero among the French peasants, because his mother was a peasant. The girl immediately covered the body with flowers and waited for others to come and carry it to the town hall, where our men received it.

213

The French Caudron G-III, used in 1915–1916 as a reconnaissance aircraft, and in 1918 as a trainer for American fliers          U. S. AIR FORCE

When Lufbery was buried on May 20, planes from the 1st Pursuit Group, led by Rickenbacker, flew over to drop flowers as the coffin was lowered into the grave. "Returning then to our vacant airdrome," Rickenbacker later recalled, "we silently faced realization that America's greatest aviator and ace of aces had been laid away to rest."

Mitchell, disciple of Hugh Trenchard, both advocated the concept of strategic bombardment, admired the courage of the men in single air combat, but realized that in order to affect the war's outcome, air force would have to be exploited according to a plan and in larger numbers. While lending tactical support to the land campaigns, the ideal employment of air power would divorce it from its land affiliations and send its planes, heavy bombers preferably, to strike at the enemy deep behind his lines. The thinking was that, if the means of making war were destroyed, so would be the enemy's will to fight. Toward this end the British formed an Independent Air Force, under command of Trenchard, which by the end of the war consisted of eleven

214

squadrons of bombers. Its D. H. 4s and D. H. 9s bombed targets in the Ruhr industrial centers as well as targets in the Rhineland. While these were successfully carried out, they were not decisive (although they did point to a devastation that would come in another war). The bombings did affect German civilian morale, embarrassed the German government and High Command and forced the withdrawal of German fighter squadrons from the war fronts.

Mitchell was finally given his opportunity to demonstrate the effect of air power in September 1918, in the battle of St.-Mihiel in which, as he himself said, he used "the greatest concentration of air power that had ever taken place and the first time in history in which an air force, cooperating with an army, was to act according to a broad strategical plan which contemplated not only facilitating the advance of the ground troops but spreading fear and consternation into the enemy's lines of communications, his replacement system and the cities behind them which supplied our foe with the sinews of war."

For this aerial assault upon the St.-Mihiel salient, Mitchell was able to put almost 1,500 aircraft (flown by Americans, British, French and Italians) into the air. Fighters served as escorts for the bombers as the sky literally swarmed with Allied aircraft. "The battle of St.-Mihiel was really over on the first day," Mitchell said, "and every objective had been accomplished." The tanks had moved into the salient and Mitchell's comment upon that phase of the operation reads today like a preview of things to come: "I was glad to see that our tanks did so well," he wrote. ". . . George Patton rode into St.-Mihiel on the back of one of his tanks, away ahead of any other ground troops in the vicinity."

Pleased with the performance of Mitchell's air force, Pershing sent his congratulations to "the Air Service of the First Army" which carried out "so successfully its dangerous and important mission. . . ."

Mitchell then moved his forces into the French sector, the Meuse-Argonne, where Foch began his tremendous assault upon the Hindenburg Line on September 26. "In addition to our own aviation," Mitchell reported, "I was getting considerable assistance from the French, two Italian Bombardment Squadrons and General Trenchard, whose British independent air force cooperated with us in bombarding the German airdromes and supply points." Although he did not have the great numbers of aircraft he had for the St.-Mihiel battle, Mitchell's air force dominated the air over the battlefield. One of the greatest operations was a bombardment of a concentration of German troops near Damvillers, a concentration which it was felt was preparing to attack the right flank of the American 3rd Corps. Mitchell requested aid from the French for this operation and received 322 Breguet bombers, each carrying ten bombs.

The French planes attacked from an altitude of 12,000 feet in V-formation; around them darted the small fighter planes to drive away any defensive German fighters. "It looked very much like a succession of flocks of swans

215

The French Salmson 2-A2, day bomber and reconnaissance aircraft which was issued to several American units during 1918          U. S. AIR FORCE

and teal ducks," Mitchell observed. "As they arrived over the target the leading squadron of from fifteen to eighteen airplanes dropped all their bombs at once. As each plane carried ten bombs, this meant one hundred and fifty bombs to each discharge.

"Within a minute after the first squadron attacked, the second one attacked and so on until twelve squadrons had delivered their bombs. While this was going on, sixty German pursuit planes were attempting in every way to get at the bombers. They came down from the direction of the sun in a succession of groups of from ten to fifteen airplanes each; the French pursuit aviation handled them beautifully. Whenever they came within reach, they were set upon by about three French airplanes to each German. Individual combats were taking place all around the bombardment ships, but not one single bombardment plane was shot down, nor was a single pursuit plane lost on the enemy side of the line; whereas we received official credit for twelve enemy planes shot down.

"Just think what it will be in the future when we attack with one, two or three thousand airplanes at one time; the effect will be decisive." Once again William Mitchell proved himself an amazing prophet. Possibly he was planning to employ such vast formations in the offensives projected for 1919, when an all-out strategic bombardment program would be unleashed upon Germany itself. Mitchell visualized one other innovation which was not put into effect, at least not in that world war. He had a plan to train infantrymen and "equip each man with a parachute, so that when we desired to make a rear attack, we could carry these men over the lines and drop them off in parachutes behind the German position."

Watching the French Breguet bombers perform recalled to Mitchell the incident of the 96th Aero Squadron, the first American bombardment squadron to see action. The unit used old French Breguets at first, then was issued new models, the 14B-2s, in July 1918. On July 10, led by the squadron commander, Maj. Harry M. Brown, six of the new Brequets took off to bomb Conflans. However, the planes became lost in the clouds and when they found an opening in the clouds, chose to land at Coblenz, mistaking it for a French city. All six planes and twelve men fell into the hands of the Germans. It rankled Mitchell when he received the following message from the Germans:

> We thank you for the fine airplanes and equipment which you have sent us, but what shall we do with the Major?

Mitchell did not answer, although he commented bitterly that "the Major" was better off in Germany at that time than he would have been with us."

The Meuse-Argonne campaign, one of the bloodiest of the war, was the last. By November 11, the Germans had given up and Mitchell was never to test his ideas for the use of air power; he would go on, even in peacetime, to fight other wars defending the efficacy of the concept of strategic air power. It would break him and he would not live to see his ideas vindicated. But even that took another, costlier, and bigger war.

The first war in the air was, in the main, a fighter pilot's war. Such theorists as Trenchard and Mitchell had begun to indoctrinate their airmen—and ground men as well—with the importance of formations, cooperation, with an almost scientific application of men and machines. There were great aerial clashes, mass dogfights that made the early battles appear like small incidents in the sky. The realization that your chances of returning home increased directly with your willingness to fly in company all but ended the era of the single aerial combat.

217

Maj. H. M. Brown and Lt. H. M. McChesney, hapless guests of the German nation after making a nearly blind landing by mistake on a German airfield. This was a German photograph which was sent to the Americans to prove that the American prisoners were well treated and in good health. When Gen. William Mitchell received the note from the Germans requesting jokingly what they should do with the Major, he decided the Major was safer in Germany than within reach of Mitchell                    U. S. SIGNAL CORPS: NATIONAL ARCHIVES

Even so, just two weeks before the Armistice was declared there occurred a classic air battle which could only have reminded even Mitchell that the individualist would ever be important in the war in the air. The bearer of this message was a twenty-four-year-old Canadian, Maj. William George Barker.

Barker had arrived in France in 1915, a machine gunner with the Canadian Mounted Rifles, Manitoba Regiment, but soon thereafter managed to be transferred to the Royal Flying Corps. He served as an observer in the old B. E. s and while serving with No. 9 Squadron shot down his first German aircraft. Barker exhibited the proper offensive spirit and was eventually sent off for flight training. He made his first solo flight following a mere 55 minutes' dual instruction. That he himself did not regard it as enough was evident, since Barker carried spare undercarriage parts tied to his plane as a

218

The French Breguet 14A-2, an all-metal two-seater reconnaissance and bombardment plane. The plane proved a worthy design and was still in use by the French Air Service until 1930. Breguets were used by American bombing and observation squadrons          U. S. SIGNAL CORPS: NATIONAL ARCHIVES

precaution against inevitability. He had a close call when he demolished an R. E. 8 while landing after an air battle.

In time both his skill as a fighter pilot and uninhibited style won Barker the doubtful recognition in the form of being posted back to England as an instructor. Barker was not very happy in this role and made it a point to let his superiors know of it both verbally and by stunting above the headquarters buildings in his Camel. Barker was sent to France with No. 28 Squadron, which fought in the Ypres sector. Barker had arrived on the 8th of October; by the end of January 1918, his score stood at nine aircraft and two balloons.

Barker then served on the Italian front, which like the Eastern Front and

219

The Fokker D-VII, one of the outstanding fighter aircraft of the First World War. Introduced to the front in the summer of 1918, the D-VII almost wrested air supremacy from the Allies. On New Year's Day, 1918, the Fokker won a fighter competition against new Aviatik, Albatros and Pfalz designs, was put into mass production and reached the fighter squadrons in July. It could climb rapidly and respond to control at high altitudes, although it was not quite as fast as the Spads and Camels.

others has received little note in air histories because of the greater drama on the Western Front. Barker himself preferred the greater action in the west, although he added considerably to his score while serving in Italy. He kept count by painting small white notches on the struts of his Camel.

In September 1918, Barker returned to England where he was supposed to command a school in aerial fighting at Hounslow. Using this as an excuse, and the fact that he had been away from the Western Front for so long, Barker had himself temporarily attached to No. 201 Squadron in France in order to study the latest fighting techniques of the Germans. He flew the latest British fighter, the hoped-for answer to the threat of the Fokker D-VII, the

Breguet bombers of the 96th Aero Squadron, A. E. F. These are planes of that unit in formation such as were led by Major Harry M. Brown, commanding officer of the 96th, on an unfortunate mission. Because of murky weather, the flight of six Breguets became lost and Lt. Hal McChesney, Brown's observer, pointed out a city through a break in the clouds. He was certain it was in German territory. Brown, however, insisted that it was a French city and led the planes, now low on fuel, in for a landing. The city turned out to be Coblenz, Germany. All the crews and six brand-new Breguets were captured by the Germans, who sent a mocking note to the Americans, asking what they should do with the Major. They knew what could be done with the planes     U. S. AIR FORCE

Sopwith "Snipe." Slightly larger than the Camel which it had been designed to replace, the Snipe was an excellent aircraft and handled beautifully despite the gyroscopic effect of the Bentley rotary engine.

During latter September and most of October, Barker served with No. 201 Squadron and brought his total up to 46 planes and 9 balloons. He was due to return to England on October 27 and had arranged to have his belongings shipped to Hounslow. Seating himself in his little Snipe, Barker took off for England.

As he climbed into the clear, brisk air Barker spotted a German Rumpler, a two-seater observation plane, circling at around 20,000 feet inside the Allied lines. His orders read that he was to return to England, but Barker found

A German Roland D-VIA, one of the designs which lost to the Fokker D-VII in the fighter competition in January 1918. It was not produced in large quantity, although it was faster than the Fokker. An interesting feature of the design is the all-wood monocoque structure of the fuselage     JARRETT COLLECTION

it impossible to ignore the Rumpler. He climbed above the Rumpler, pulled up behind it and with a short burst sent the German plane down without wings.

Barker then was painfully surprised when he himself was struck by an explosive bullet that shattered his right thigh. A Fokker D-VII had dropped down on him as Barker had watched the Rumpler fall into the Mormal Forest. Despite the pain, and the fact that he could not move his right foot to kick the rudder, Barker brought the Snipe around and shot down the Fokker, which burned and twisted its way to the ground.

To his further surprise Barker found himself in the middle of an entire German formation of Fokkers, a triplane and D-VIIs—according to some counts no less than sixty enemy aircraft. Instead of diving his Snipe to the safety of any nearby airdrome, Barker for some reason chose instead to remain and fight. He was wounded and outnumbered sixty to one but he stayed.

Soon Barker's Snipe was the target for swarms of Fokkers as Spandau slugs streamed at him from every direction. He himself was wounded in the left thigh, although within moments after he was attacked he had flamed two more German planes. To make himself a difficult target, Barker slammed the Snipe around the sky as much as he could; he even fainted from loss of blood and undoubtedly threw off the aim of the attacking Fokkers when his plane fell out of control. The rush of air revived Barker and he pulled the plane out of the spin. He had now abandoned all thought of surviving the battle and tried to ram the attacking Fokkers which scattered. With his guns Barker sent another down in flames.

Maj. William George Barker in Italy. The plane is a Camel    JARRETT COLLECTION

A burst of German machine-gun fire shot away Barker's left elbow; he fainted again, recovered, returned to the fight—and another Fokker went down burning.

But loss of blood and the pain took their toll; both legs and his left arm were useless. Barker's only chance lay in breaking out of the box the Fokkers had formed around his Snipe. He broke through the formation but not without having his fuel tank shot away from under his seat. In a haze, Barker switched to the auxiliary tank and headed his shredded Snipe for the British lines. Only half conscious and with practically no control over his plane, Barker brought the Snipe down behind the British positions. The plane came down at full speed, crashed, left splinters along its landing path and then turned over. When some Highlanders reached the wrecked plane they were

223

The 1918 Sopwith Snipe, the last of the rotary-powered fighting planes. It was in a Snipe that William Barker single-handedly took on sixty German aircraft in a dogfight. The Snipe's handling characteristics, particularly its maneuverability, enabled Barker to shoot down four German planes before he himself was shot down                                                             JARRETT COLLECTION

amazed to find the pilot still alive—although his nose had been broken in the crash landing.

Barker was unconscious for days, but he did recover, received the Victoria Cross from the hands of King George. He also learned that in the two weeks during which he lingered between life and death, the Great War had ended.

If the airmen did not contribute materially to the final outcome, they had proved that the air weapon could be decisive if properly employed. They had also proved they were men of unique courage. With few exceptions they fought with unusual gallantry and without the savagery that marked the battle

A Spad of the 94th Aero Squadron, flown by Samuel Kaye. This is a post-Armistice photo, for such flamboyant decorations were not permitted during the war

U. S. AIR FORCE

on the ground. They had managed to bring a kind of dignity to the indignity of war; they had managed to preserve human individuality in a war of mass attrition and waste. When they fell, their value was above that of the sparrows and their fall was noted. Their tragedy lay in their personal sacrifice, freely given, which their leaders wasted or did not understand until it was too late; nor were they aware of the fact that the "war to end all wars" had only been a prelude.

With the coming of peace thousands of aircraft were junked. So were many of the lessons learned during the war about air power U. S. AIR FORCE

ÉTABLISSEMENT CINÉMATOGRAPHIQUE DES ARMÉES

German "atrocities" as reported in propaganda releases in 1915. One shows a supposed crucifixion of a Canadian soldier; the other German doctors removing the eyes of Allied prisoners. Babies were said to have been brutally murdered in Belgium and defenseless maidens raped. It was admitted after the war that such reports were either untrue or grossly exaggerated FRENCH EMBASSY

# *Appendix*

*How these curiosities would be quite forgott,
did not such idle fellows as I putt them downe!*

—JOHN AUBREY: *Brief Lives,*
with an affectionate nod to
Ira Gershwin, Gent.

# Bibliography

The vast literature devoted to the aerial operations of the First World War breaks down, roughly, into three main categories: the personal narrative, history and the technical. Most autobiographical or biographical accounts were published shortly after the war's end; the histories came shortly after. The best of the technical books are a quite recent phenomena which indicate a great interest in the aircraft to the point of specialization. Some of the early biographies are models of highly romanticized tales, long on storytelling and short on fact. The more recent technical books are just the opposite, which is not always an asset. The careful research of latter-day enthusiasts, particularly the members of the Society of World War 1 Aero Historians who publish their findings in the excellent magazine *Cross and Cockade Journal,* has helped to establish certain facts, diminish myths and to place many an incident in proper historical perspective. Such attention, however, lavished upon the war by many who never experienced it, intrudes an aura of romanticism for all the factual preoccupation. And the cause of World War I aerial scholarship will be better served by such fine books as Dr. Douglas Robinson's masterly *The Zeppelin in Combat* than arguments over whether or not Richthofen flew an all-red triplane at all times or only some of the time. There is a fine line between scholarship and nit-picking.

Some of the books listed here may not satisfy all the demands of scholarship, but they do help to recreate the immediate atmosphere of the times as revealed in the personal reminiscences of the men who experienced the first war in the air, although without the full awareness of what it all meant historically. The ability to fly a plane does not make a man a historian; but his having taken part in an important event makes his views interesting and even valuable.

That they believed themselves to be involved in Something Big is evident from the diaries and letters written by the fliers at the time.

The books marked with an asterisk (*) are out of print. Let the buyer beware; specialist book dealers know how much the books are in demand, their rarity and can read the gleam in the collector's eye down to the last dollar. Some of the prices charged for rather poor books are amazing—There is a biography of Frank Luke, for example, which generally fetches $20 or more; the two-volume history of the Lafayette Flying Corps by Hall and Nordhoff may bring in $150. It is a fine job, but the price is steep indeed. Happily, more recent books now in print and in preparation will present the story of the first war in the air more completely than ever before and with a good deal less slipshod attention to the facts.

The following are among the books which proved most helpful in researching this one:

  \* Bishop, William A., *Winged Warfare*. George H. Doran Co., New York, 1918.

  \* Bordeaux, Henry, *Guynemer, Knight of the Air*. Yale University Press, New Haven, 1918

  Bruce, J. M., *British Aeroplanes 1914–1918*. Putnam, London, 1957.

  \* Chapman, John Jay, ed., *Victor Chapman's Letters From France*. The Macmillan Co., New York, 1919.

  \* Driggs, Laurence La Tourette, *Heroes of Aviation*. Little, Brown and Co., Boston, 1918.

  Gray, Peter and Thetford, Owen, *German Aircraft of the First World War*. Putnam, London, 1962.

  Hadow, G. W. and Grosz, Peter M., *The German Giants*. Putnam, London, 1962.

  Hall, James M. and Nordhoff, Charles B., *The Lafayette Flying Corps*. Houghton Mifflin Co., Boston; to be reissued by Kennikat Press, Inc., Port Washington, N. Y., 1964.

  \* Jones, H. A. and Raleigh, Walter, *The War in the Air* (nine volumes). Oxford University Press, Oxford, 1931.

  \* Lewis, Cecil, *Sagittarius Rising*. Harcourt, Brace and Co., New York, 1936.

  McKee, Alexander, *The Friendless Sky*. William Morrow and Co., New York, 1964.

  Mitchell, William, *Memoirs of World War I*. Random House, New York, 1960.

  Nowarra, H. J. and Brown, Kimbrough, *Von Richthofen and the "Flying Circus."* Harleyford Publications Ltd., Letchworth, Herts. (England), 1958.

  Parsons, Edwin C., *I Flew with the Lafayette Escadrille* (originally entitled *The Great Adventure*). E. C. Seale and Co., Indianapolis, 1963.

  Reynolds, Quentin, *They Fought For the Sky*. Rinehart and Co., Inc., New York, 1957.

  \* Richthofen, Manfred von, *Red Battle Flyer*. Robert M. McBride and Co., New York, 1918.

  Rickenbacker, Edward V., *Fighting the Flying Circus*. Frederick Stokes Co., New York, 1919; to be reissued by Doubleday & Co., 1965.

  Robertson, Bruce, ed., *Air Aces of the 1914–1918 War*. Harleyford Publications Ltd., Letchworth, Herts. (England), 1959.

  Robinson, Douglas, *The Zeppelin in Combat*. G. T. Foulis and Co., Ltd., London, 1962.

  \* Springs, Elliot White (the author is generally listed as "Anon."), *War Birds*. George H. Doran Company, New York, 1926.

Thetford, O. G. and Riding, E. J., *Aircraft of the 1914–1918 War.* Harleyford Publications, Ltd., Letchworth, Herts. (England), 1954.

Whitehouse, Arch, *Decisive Air Battles of the First World War.* Duell, Sloan and Pearce, New York, 1963.

# *The Aces*

The following tabulation of the aces of the First World War is based on more or less official scores; if not official, at least they are accepted by students of the period. Although Richthofen's tally adds up to eighty, not all of these victories were officially confirmed, even in German records. It will be noted that German, British and French scores are very high, as compared with say Belgian, Italian and Austrian. The latter were comparatively quiet fronts, at least in the air. British scores might even be higher but because many of their "kills" fell behind German lines, they were not always accredited. Probably the most important point a listing such as this makes is that so much emphasis was placed upon aerial warfare as a competitive sport; it should be emphasized that each number following the name of the ace, while representing his victory list, also may have represented a man who died. The ten top-scoring airmen of each country, and their kills, were as follows:

*Austria-Hungary*

| | |
|---|---|
| Godwin Brunowski | 40 |
| Julius Arigi | 32 |
| Frank Linke-Crawford | 30 |
| Benno von Fernbrugg | 29 |
| Josef Kiss | 19 |
| Franz Gräser | 16 |
| Stefen Fejes | 15 |
| Eugen Bönsch | 15 |
| Kurt Gruber | 14 |
| Ernst Strohschneider | 14 |

*Belgium*

| | |
|---|---|
| Willy Coppens | 37 |
| Andre de Meulemeester | 11 |
| Edmond Thieffry | 10 |
| Fernand Jacquet | 7 |
| Jan Olieslagers | 6 |
| G. Kervyn de Lettenhove | 4 |
| L. Robin | 4 |
| E. Hage | 3 |
| M. Benselin | 2 |
| P. Braun | 2 |

*Great Britain*

| | |
|---|---|
| Edward Mannock | 73 |
| William A. Bishop | 72 |
| Raymond Collishaw | 60 |
| James T. McCudden | 57 |
| Anthony Beauchamp-Proctor | 54 |
| Donald R. MacLaren | 54 |
| William G. Barker | 53 |
| Robert A. Little | 47 |
| Philip F. Fullard | 46 |
| George E. McElroy | 46 |

*France*

| | |
|---|---|
| René Fonck | 75 |
| Georges Guynemer | 54 |
| Charles Nungesser | 45 |
| Georges Madon | 41 |
| Maurice Boyau | 35 |
| Michel Coiffard | 34 |
| Jean Bourjade | 28 |
| Armand Pinsard | 27 |
| René Dorme | 23 |
| Gabriel Guérin | 23 |

## Germany

| | |
|---|---|
| Manfred von Richthofen | 80 |
| Ernst Udet | 62 |
| Erich Loewenhardt | 53 |
| Werner Voss | 48 |
| Fritz Rumey | 45 |
| Rudolph Berthold | 44 |
| Paul Baumer | 43 |
| Josef Jacobs | 41 |
| Bruno Loerzer | 41 |
| Oswald Boelcke | 40 |

## Italy

| | |
|---|---|
| Francesco Baracca | 34 |
| Silvio Scaroni | 26 |
| Pier Piccio | 24 |
| Flavio Baracchini | 21 |
| Fulco di Calabria | 20 |
| Marziale Cerutti | 17 |
| Ferruccio Ranza | 17 |
| Luigi Olivari | 12 |
| Giovanni Ancillotto | 11 |
| Antonio Reali | 11 |

## Russia

| | |
|---|---|
| Alexander A. Kazakov | 17 |
| Paul v. d'Arqueeff | 15 |
| Alexander P. de Seversky | 13 |
| Ivan Smirnoff | 12 |
| Mikhail Safonov | 11 |
| Boris Sergievsky | 11 |
| Eduard Tomson | 11 |
| Evgraph Kruten | 7 |
| Grigori Suk | 7 |
| Ivan Orlov | 6 |

## United States

| | |
|---|---|
| Edward V. Rickenbacker | 26 |
| Frank Luke, Jr. | 21 |
| Raoul Lufbery | 17 |
| George A. Vaughn, Jr. | 13 |
| Field E. Kindley | 12 |
| David E. Putnam | 12 |
| Elliot White Springs | 12 |
| Reed G. Landis | 10 |
| Jacques M. Swaab | 10 |
| L. A. Hamilton | 9 |

# *Index*